*With
Courage and
Common Sense*

With Courage and Common Sense

Memoirs from the
Older Women's Legacy
Circles

Edited and with
Introductions by
Susan Wittig Albert
and
Dayna Finet

Foreword by
Liz Carpenter

University of Texas Press
Austin

First edition, 2003

Requests for permission to reproduce material from this work should be
sent to Permissions, University of Texas Press, Box 7819, Austin, TX
78713-7819.

⊚ The paper used in this book meets the minimum requirements of
ANSI/NISO Z39.48-1992 (R1997) (Permanence of Paper).

LIBRARY OF CONGRESS CATALOGING-IN-PUBLICATION DATA

With courage and common sense : memoirs from the Older Women's
Legacy Circles / edited and with introductions by Susan Wittig Albert
and Dayna Finet ; foreword by Liz Carpenter.

     p.   cm.
Includes bibliographical references.
ISBN 0-292-70549-2 (alk. paper)
ISBN 0-292-70188-8 (pbk. : alk. paper)
 1. Aged women—Texas—Biography. 2. Women—Texas—Biogra-
phy. 3. Autobiographies—Texas. 4. Texas—Biography. 5. Biogra-
phy as a literary form. 6. Biography—20th century. I. Albert, Susan
Wittig. II. Finet, Dayna, 1956–
CT3260.W623   2003
976.4'06'0922—dc21

                                        2002156543

To the women of the

Story Circle Network

without whose help and support

these stories,

and many others,

would be forever lost

Contents

CHAPTER FOUR.

Family: *Grandmother and the Pirates* 85

CHAPTER FIVE.

Love: *'Til We Meet Again* 101

CHAPTER SIX.

Loss: *The Strength to Survive* 115

Living Fully: *I Still Had My Two Dollars* 133

Witness: *Ordinary Lives, Extraordinary Events* 149

CHAPTER NINE.

Legacies: *"I Wish You Could Have Known My Grandma"* 171

Foreword

Liz Carpenter

For women who have been in the last two centuries' struggle for equality, walking through the Women's Museum is an emotional experience. I found myself weeping and cheering. Everyone should take this trip, ideally with a young woman—a daughter, a sister, a granddaughter.

Nicely housed in the renovated Administration Building at Dallas's Fair Park, the Women's Museum opened in October 2000. It's the first and only comprehensive museum of women's history in the United States. Exhibits throughout the museum acknowledge the achievements of America's most respected and celebrated women. But along with these, a visitor will find the humbler tales of women who made their contributions with no public (and maybe no private) recognition at all. At an array of computer stations, museum visitors can write their own life stories: each individual's experience contributes to the collective memory.

We are all storytellers, and our best tales come from real life. I've made a living by talking and writing for almost six decades now, beginning as a young reporter in Washington during the final years of the FDR presidency and now, in part, as a memoirist fortunate to enjoy an audience for the recollections of my eventful life. Countless women have been less lucky. We'll never know how many women's stories have been lost because they weren't thought valuable. Like the Women's Museum, *With Courage and Common Sense* makes it a point to honor the women whose stories might have gone untold.

Many of the women whose writing you'll read in this book came from Texas, and their stories evoke imagery long taken as typically Texan. Eula Rae McCown tells how her skill with a pistol enchanted her husband-to-be. Erin Colleen Moore remembers how she saddled up and rode along on cattle drives. Other women came to Texas from somewhere else. They're Texans now, but in their writing, memories of other homes linger too. But for the circumstance of war, Mathilda Mimun might have remained in Tunisia, Sarah Lichtman in Poland, Jean Wyllys and Eileen Titus in England. Grace Schmitt writes of going back, with her son and granddaughter, to find the Greenwich Village apartment building where she'd grown up.

Much of the time our society stereotypes and dismisses old women as ridiculous, troublesome, irrelevant, and (worst of all) boring. These memoirs contradict the assumptions. The women who wrote them have experienced solid, hearty lives, with a characteristic vitality enduring into old age. Writing about her work as a professor at American University, Faye Kelly remembers the man's world that was academia and the first efforts by female faculty to move the profession toward gender equity. A memoir by Dolores Muhich tells how she and her traveling companions escaped the 1968 Soviet invasion of Czechoslovakia. Jeanie Forsyth writes about her blistering three-week midsummer Outward Bound excursion at Big Bend as a member of the "geriatric patrol." The fullness of these women's lives also shows in their stories about meaningful small events. Marji Smith writes about the sympathetic vet who accepted office cleaning as payment for doctoring her injured puppy, freeing up her last two dollars to spend on flour tortillas and honey, enough to last two days.

No one can live six decades or more without facing hardship and loss. In this book, memoirs recall the collective ordeals— the economic despair, the wars, the assassinations—interpreting these momentous public events as they were privately experienced. Perhaps because of happenstance or because it's a generational trait, these writers often locate the small incidents of good found even in adversity. Jean Leonard's Pearl Harbor memoir features the coincidence of that infamous day with a fondly remembered Sweet Sixteen surprise party and birthday concert at Radio City Music Hall. There are stories of personal trauma that must have taken courage to retell. Ruby Bishop writes that "no child should witness" what she saw as her mother descended into schizophrenia and forced institutionalization. Selah Rose's memoir counts all that she gave up to free herself from an abusive forty-year marriage. More important: it concludes that her renewed, true-to-self life, with its fresh anticipation of the future, has been worth the cost.

Twice events have called on me to remake my life, so I have some experience with renewal. In 1974 my husband Leslie died, and Washington, where we had savored living together for more than thirty years, no longer felt right. I returned to Texas, settled into a home on a hill overlooking Austin, and filled my days with writing and speaking, feminist causes, and friends who brought the zest back into my life. Then, in 1991, my brother Tom died and his three teenagers came to live with me. I wasn't sure I had the resources—physical, emotional, financial—to deal with this unplanned return to parenthood. I felt reluctant to sacrifice my work, my friends, and my freedom. But I could not fail to take care of those children. The challenges of seventy-something surrogate motherhood were hard. And they convinced me that I could handle the surprises that life has left for me still.

Firsthand insight into ordinary people's lives and witness to the monumental events of last century, these memoirs contribute to history. The memoirs are a valuable legacy, but not the only one. These memoirs teach us, but subtly: they don't tell us how to live, but rather, how the women who wrote them lived. Theirs is the power of example. Simple and unpretentious, the writing in this book is endowed with truth and meaning.

Acknowledgments

This collection of memoirs has been a project of the Story Circle Network, and from the beginning, its success has depended on the contributions of a great many women. It was the generous funding provided by the Sisters of Charity of the Incarnate Word of Houston, Texas, that made the OWL (Older Women's Legacy) Circle Project possible. Other major contributors included Sister Hannah O'Donoghue and Mary Jane Marks, who helped shape the grant proposal and supported other phases of the project; Catherine Cogburn, who managed the office, scheduled workshops, and produced the booklets for each group; the facilitators who led the workshops; and the participants themselves, who were the life and spirit of the project. Dayna Finet made the original selections for this collection and drafted introductions. Theresa May, at the University of Texas Press, offered suggestions and encouragement at several crucial moments. And the women who served on the Story Circle Board of Directors from 1998 to the present gave generous gifts of time, energy, and love in support of the activities and projects of this small but ambitious organization, including this book. I am personally grateful to each of you.

Susan Wittig Albert, Ph.D.
President, Story Circle Network

Introduction

Women are born storytellers. Like all good stories, the tales they tell about their lives exhibit a vast complexity of plots and subplots, rich ironies and subtle ambiguities, stunning setbacks and happy endings. When these stories are shared, they promote the most satisfying of human experiences: recognition, connection, understanding. In true story sharing, teller and hearer meet at the intersection of their experience, and both are enriched. And like any valuable legacy, women's stories are handed down through their families' generations, enriching the future with an understanding of the past.

This collection of women's stories comes from a fortunate coincidence of purpose and opportunity that grew into the Older Women's Legacy Circle (OWL Circle) Project. Beginning in 1998, the OWL Circle Project created and conducted forty-eight free guided memoir-writing workshops for women over sixty, held mostly in and around Austin, Texas. By its conclusion in late 2000, the grant-funded phase of the project had supported the writing of some four thousand short memoirs by almost five hundred writers—a substantial collection of memories and stories.

Women's story sharing is an activity that is not always valued in our culture. In fact, it is often considered, as the literary scholar Linda Wagner-Martin points out, as merely gossip. Contrasting men's and women's storytelling, she adds, "When men talk together, even though they discuss golf scores, the conversation is business. When women talk together, they are criticized and patronized, as are their narratives" (Wagner-Martin 1994).

It was a group of women talking together who conceived and developed the OWL Circle. Early in 1998, board members of the Story Circle Network (SCN) were making plans for the coming year. SCN, a Texas-based nonprofit organization devoted to encouraging women to write about their lives, had been established not long before. To encourage women's personal storytelling, the organization published the quarterly *Story Circle Journal,* maintained a web site, supported two chapters and a number of circles around the United States, sponsored workshops and special events, and had already begun thinking about its first national conference. The board was also exploring other possible ways of fulfilling its missions: working with girls in schools, with incarcerated women, with breast cancer survivors, with older women.

It was in the context of discussions about the need to preserve older women's life stories that the OWL Circle Project began. Board member Mary Jane Marks, who was active in various senior organizations in the Austin area, thought that those organizations would enthusiastically support a women's life-writing program, especially if the cost to the participants was low. Another board member, Sister Hannah O'Donoghue, suggested that SCN might apply for funding to her order, the Sisters of Charity of the Incarnate Word, so that the workshops could be offered without charge. Within a few weeks, the grant proposal had been written. It was funded a few months later, and the project began.

At the time, a few guided autobiography programs for seniors were being conducted around the country (Birren and Deutchman 1991), but none involved only older women—and the women planning this project insisted that it be a "women only" activity. For one thing, their own experience and observation led them to believe that many women have learned to inhibit their storytelling in the presence of men, perhaps for fear of revealing too much, perhaps because they sense that men view women's stories as valueless. On the other hand, they also knew from experience that women share even intimate details about their lives more readily with other women. The planners also believed that men's stories and women's stories are fundamentally different. Women's stories often lack the cohesive, forward-moving narrative line that characterizes the stories of men: the "and then . . . and then . . . and finally . . ." that pulls the story forward along its linear plot, from one adventure to the next. A woman storyteller tends to circle around her subject, to hover. She is often captured by a detail, an emotion, a moment. Her stories are more associative than linear, more character focused and less plot driven.

The author and scholar Shari Benstock (1991) has described the stories of women's lives as a metaphorical fishnet: all strings and empty space, the told and the untold, coexistent. It is like a skein of yarn: tangled, knotted, frayed, but still useful, its creative potential still intact. Mary Catherine Bateson (1990) describes women's lives and their life stories as an improvisational art, discontinuous and interrupted; like braided laces, the strands of new stories are continually interwoven with threads of the old.

The OWL Circle planning group thought of women's life stories as a quilt, pieced out of fragments of lived experience —some vividly recalled, others faded—cut into meaningful shapes, and assembled, with a unique and creative vision, into new designs rich with a lifetime's memory and meaning. As they come together to quilt, women have traditionally joined companionship with creation, not just of something beautiful, but of something valuable and valued for its handcraftedness, something useful to be handed down to children, to grandchildren, through the passing generations. Quilts testify to the experience of individual women, situated as they are in a particular time and place and made for a specific purpose, and yet they testify to the experience of all women. Quilts are something women understand. The writers who participated in the OWL Circle Project could see that their stories were like quilts.

And they very much liked the idea of sharing their stories, just as they remembered their mothers and aunts and grandmothers sitting down to quilt together.

From the outset, the OWL Circle planners recognized that they would be working with a generation of women trained to reticence, women who had been taught not to make too much of themselves, to think of their experiences as of little value. They knew that they would have to find a way to encourage participants to write. "Many women I know have kept journals," Mary Jane Marks says, "but when the suggestion is made to share or publish, they deny their own right to do so. I believed that this project could help release some of those stories. Just the experience of having someone listen and care means a great deal." Faye Kelly, a retired professor whose stories appear in Chapters Three and Eight, observed women's reluctance to write about their lives—in part, she thought, because they had learned their cultural lesson well: women's lives just aren't worth writing about.

> I was really surprised how women of my generation have said, "Well, I haven't done anything in my life to write about." And I've tried to convince them that their children and grandchildren and even great-grandchildren would be very happy to have any information. After all, our generation has experienced as much change and as much chaos as any other one in our history. We all had to go through the Depression. We all had to go through World War II, and through the Korean War. And then our sons had to go to Vietnam. Just purely the act of living has changed so much in my lifetime that my grandchildren can't even conceive of some of the things that we did not have. Indoor plumbing, to begin with. And when we first got electricity it was one light bulb on a long string hanging down in the middle of the room, and we were thrilled to have it. I remember getting a telephone. We had only one in the house—that was it.

But to get it out of them and get them to put it down on paper—after all, writing is hard work. It's a very rewarding activity, but it's still hard work.

Before members of the planning group developed the workshops themselves, they articulated an ethic that would consciously honor the dignity and worth of each participant and create a climate of caring and respect through nonjudgmental listening, uncritical acceptance, and complete confidentiality. No woman would have to worry about what people might think, they decided, or fear that someone would carry tales outside the group. Each woman could say no at any time: participation in all writing and speaking activities during the workshops would be voluntary. And in order to give the women the freedom to look deep within themselves, no men would be allowed —particularly husbands (with one exception: at the Conley-Guerrero Senior Activity Center in Austin, OWL Circle women voted unanimously to allow a longtime, trusted male friend to join their group).

The planning group turned next to the practical tasks of designing the basic structure and administrative procedures for the workshops. Over the next several months, they created workbooks for participants and support material for facilitators, scheduled workshop sites, selected and trained workshop facilitators, and developed ways to advertise the project and recruit participants.

Initially, the memoir groups (usually eight to ten participants) met four times, weekly, biweekly, or (in one case) monthly. Each meeting was two and a half hours long, with a break in the middle. The workshop facilitator began by introducing the two workbook topics and writing exercises for that session, one before the break and one after. Participants wrote for twenty to thirty minutes on each topic, then were given the opportunity to read their stories aloud to the group. Many began by struggling to produce only a few awkward sentences. But as they became more comfortable and more deeply engaged with their memories, their writing facility increased and they wrote at great length and with greater ease and enthusiasm, often surprising themselves with the quantity and quality of their work. Reading aloud proved to be a more difficult challenge, but it, too, became easier and more rewarding as the work was met with acceptance and (often) applause. Before closing the meeting, the facilitator directed the women's attention to the additional writing topics in the workbook and encouraged them to write between sessions. Some of the longer stories in this collection were composed in this way.

To affirm the value of the women's memoirs and give them permanency, stories from each of the workshops were collected and compiled into a booklet, five copies of which were distributed free to each participant in that workshop. This publication was an important and popular feature of the project, for it gave every woman the opportunity to see some of her writing in print. "Most of the participants had the feeling that their stories weren't 'good enough' to be published," says Project Director Catherine Cogburn. "So the booklets played a critical role, boosting their self-confidence and assuring them that their writing, and their experience, was important and valuable. They were delighted when they got their copies of the booklets and immediately shared them with friends and family."

Another valuable feature of the project was the OWL Circle Workbook, inserted into a three-ring binder, which was created by a team of experienced teachers, psychotherapists, and curriculum development experts.[1] Cogburn remarked on its importance: "Since each participant received her own workbook, she could look ahead and think about the topics for the next session—an important incentive for attendance. She could also insert her own work into the binder, personalizing it. Many women commented that the workbook made writing easy and fun."

Supplied without charge to each participant, the workbook provided the framework, rationale, and writing topics for each workshop session, as well as between-session writing topics, graphic organizers with exercises to help writers structure their recollections, and suggestions for sharing stories. All of the topics and exercises were designed to encourage women to write about themselves, not about other people. There was no particular focus on writing technique.

The first draft of the workbook was tested during a preliminary round of thirteen workshops held between January and May 1999. It was evaluated by participants and facilitators, revised, and retested in subsequent workshops. Because participants and facilitators wanted more time for writing and sharing, the number of workshop sessions was increased from four to five. Participants disliked two of the topics, or found them irrelevant, so these were eliminated and new topics suggested by participants were added, as well as new memory prompts and organizers. The revised workbook also contained a new bibliography on women's life writing and the "OWL Circle Agreement," the guide to workshop conduct. The Facilitators' Manual, which was designed to enable even an untrained leader to successfully conduct the workshops, was also revised to provide additional suggestions for workshop management.

Facilitators came mostly from the membership of the Story Circle Network and received payment for their work. They made an invaluable contribution to the process. "They encouraged participants to look deeply into their experience, to write without fear, and to share without embarrassment," Cogburn said. "Their commitment was a vital key to the success of these groups." Mary Jane Marks, who initially helped to select and train the facilitators, urged them not to instruct the writers, but to encourage and empower them. "The important thing was to facilitate the group's work," Marks said, "not to teach those whose experience was the teacher."

Although the workbook provided a basic structure, facilitators and participants together often modified activities to fit the unique combination of personalities and temperaments within a given OWL Circle group. Groups decided to alter, shorten, lengthen, or skip topics. Some groups suggested topics in response to ongoing events in the lives of workshop participants. Nearly all the participants could write without physical assistance, but a small number of women required assistance or extra writing time to accommodate conditions of aging such as impaired vision and hearing or arthritis, and the session structure was altered when necessary to meet their needs.

Within the workshops, reading aloud was considered an integral part of the writing process. These readings often struck an echoing chord in the hearts and minds of the other participants, evoking deeply felt memories, both happy and painful. One facilitator, Linda Watkins, explained how the hearers often "found themselves" in another woman's story:

> Part of the time, the women felt that this really was not fun. And that's true. It was hard work, emotionally, to deal with some of these issues, but important. And I would keep saying, "This is not fun; this is *important*. This is an opportunity to understand better the meaning and purpose and direction of your life." Of course, the act of writing is wonderful—just to begin to search your past and put that down on paper in a meaningful way. But add to that the experience of reading it aloud. That gets you at a cellular level in a way that just the writing doesn't. When you hear yourself speak the words, they become part of an internal reality. And then to have a setting in which you share that with others and listen to their stories is enormously engaging and rewarding. Women find themselves in the other person's story. Too often we feel isolated and alone. "I'm the only one who's experienced this," and "Nobody understands." But when women come together and share their experiences in a safe, loving, warm environment, it's an absolutely life-changing endeavor.

The workshops took place at a variety of locations, most of them arranged through the Austin senior organizations. Some groups met in the living rooms of facilitators or participants. Others met in municipal senior activity centers, in churches and synagogues, and in public and private retirement residences. A division of one of Austin's largest healthcare organizations, the

Seton Good Health School, hosted workshops at several of its facilities. Cathy Butler, the school's director, remarked that the workshops were a good fit with Seton's holistic approach to wellness:

> The OWL-Circle memoir workshops were in perfect alignment with what we do in the Good Health School, and totally congruent with what I already knew about body, mind, and spirit integration. I liked the idea of storytelling, and we were starting to do a lot of work to encourage people with journaling, understanding that self-revelation can resolve issues and help people make sense of what's happened in their lives.

Self-revelation through personal writing can indeed play an important role in an individual's psychological and physical health, according to the psychologist James Pennebaker (1997), who has been evaluating the impact of personal writing on the health and well-being of college students for over twenty years. Pennebaker's respected and groundbreaking research suggests that suppressing a difficult experience is likely to make us ill, while writing about it enhances healing. And when the writing becomes a regular feature of our day or week, the benefits seem to accelerate. "Writing," he says, "can be an avenue to that interior place where . . . we can confront traumas and put them to rest."

According to Louise DeSalvo (1999), writing can be a kind of "symbolic repair," a way to put traumatic events and feelings into perspective. As we write about experience, we reenter it, gaining a helpful understanding and clarity, and can then release it and go on to something else. In what DeSalvo calls "healing narrative," we learn how to observe ourselves, how to recognize productive and nonproductive behaviors, how to reframe experience and understand it. In writing, we give coherence to the often disordered fragments of memory; through writing, we become absorbed in the activity of creation. And when we share our written narratives with caring, nonjudgmental listeners, the healing powers of writing are intensified. "How Telling Our Stories Transforms Our Lives" is the subtitle of DeSalvo's book, and it was an underlying theme of the OWL Circle memoir workshops.

Older women, especially, may benefit from the process of writing down important personal experiences and sharing them with empathetic listeners. Older men's stories are often validated by family, community, and culture—witness the proliferation of personal stories about the wars of this century that have been collected, published, and aired on television in recent years. But such opportunities are rare for older women, whose lives have been largely focused on home and family. As they write and talk about their experiences within an environment of support and recognition, they may be able to more fully acknowledge their own personal worth and the importance of their contributions to family and community—acknowledgments that may help to combat the depression that so frequently afflicts older women.

Writing about their lives gives women an authority of voice that comes from self-knowledge: "We're heard when we speak out of our understanding of our own experience," according to the autobiographer Jill Ker Conway (1998). The author bell hooks tells us that women's autobiographical writing both releases us from our past and reunites us with it. "The act of writing one's autobiography is a way to find again that aspect of self and experience that may no longer be an actual part of one's life but is a living memory shaping and informing the present," (hooks 1999). For many women today, the ongoing re-creation of self is both a requirement and a reward of aging. Carolyn Heilbrun writes, "For women who have awakened to new possibilities in middle age, or who were born into the current women's movement and have escaped the usual rhythms of the once traditional female existence, the last third of life is likely to require new attitudes and new courage" (Heilbrun 1988). As a creative practice, life writing can play a vital role in sustaining a woman's healthy maturity.

Although the facilitators and participants felt that the memoir workshops were unequivocally successful, the OWL Circle Project organizers were disappointed in at least one aspect of their work. Despite a serious commitment of will and effort, only one workshop included a substantial number of women from nonwhite and less affluent populations. Allison Downey facilitated that workshop, held at Austin's Conley-Guerrero Senior Activity Center. As a University of Texas graduate student, Downey had staged a performance based on the life stories of people she met at Conley-Guerrero. Through that work, she had established a rapport that enabled her to propose an OWL Circle workshop to the center, and she had developed the intercultural skills needed to make the workshop rewarding for them. Downey's comments here reflect both the challenges and rewards that might have been met in a more demographically diverse life-writing project:

> I would say that anybody working to promote a true representation of the population should either be from the population or should have a very strong connection with it. It's fascinating for me to see what their struggles were. But if they don't want to share, then it's manipulative of me to try to get them to do it. I had to prove I had a reason for being there and wasn't interested just in getting what I needed and leaving. [It worked] because I already had a relationship with them. I had worked with them. They trusted me. They're my friends. Otherwise I would have just been the white lady coming in trying to steal people's stories.

By fall of 2000, the two-year grant-funded phase of the OWL Circle Project was over. "Final? How sad, that word," wrote one participant on her evaluation questionnaire. For the Story Circle Network, however, the project was not over; it moved into a second phase as the Network began to offer the OWL Circle Workbook and Facilitators' Manual to women's groups around the country. [For information about the current program, see "About Story Circle Network" at the end of the book.] The project was not over, either, for many of the women who participated in the original program. Several workshop groups continued to meet for many months; others are meeting still, their members continuing to write and read and share with each other. And in yet other cases, individual women continued to write alone, finding a new and more significant purpose in setting down their memoirs. Faye Kelly writes:

> [The OWL Circle Project] was the beginning for me of writing my life story. Of course, I had wonderful intentions to do it for years, and I've always been interested in language and words. But I just never got around to it. Now, I write when I feel like writing and whenever there's something that I want to put down that I remember. I have a few tricks that stimulate me to think about things, and when I do think of something, I write it down in a little notebook—in there, I also put quotes and things that I hear that will stimulate me to write later. At night when I'm not able to sleep and I think of anything that's concrete enough, I write it down on the pad I keep by the bed. If you don't put something down then, it's gone, usually, and you may not ever get it back again. I think about revisions that I can do. Usually I can revise in my mind and then when I get back to it, I can write it down quite easily. And I'm trying to get my children, and certainly my grandchildren, to ask me questions or remember for me incidents that I might not have thought of and that they'd like to hear about.

The creative act of writing about their lives in an environment that honored and authenticated their efforts inspired a real, if sometimes intangible, transformation for the women who participated in OWL Circle.

One such transformation occurred for Marj Batlan, a woman who had gathered a group of her friends to participate in the OWL Circle workshop led by Judith Helburn. Helburn herself must tell the story, because Marj Batlan died halfway through the sessions.

When I started the Older Women's Legacy Circle in February 1999, Marj Batlan came and brought with her seventeen other women. And then, very suddenly, that vivacious woman was gone.

The day of the third class was also the day of Marj's funeral, so I cancelled class. When I arrived at the synagogue, the family was in the small chapel. Mort, Marj's husband, came up to me and hugged me. He said that in the previous two weeks, he would get up about 7 A.M. and Marj would be at her desk, writing furiously. Somehow, a part of her sensed that she would soon be gone. She was lucid for about eighteen hours between her first stroke and the final massive one. She told her daughter-in-law that night that she had to tell her stories for her grandchildren. And as Marj was dying, she was writing with her fingers on the bed sheet.

You never know how much what you do affects others. I'm still awestruck at what the family told me, how much they appreciated the OWL Circle, what a catalyst it had been for Marj. And what a privilege for me to have participated.

Marj Batlan's story may be dramatic, but it is in many ways typical of the responses of these women memoirists. Once they began to feel the power of their stories, they were possessed by a great urgency to set them down. "I want to tell it before it's all gone," one woman said. "I never thought it was important before. Now I do." Their families are grateful. "I think the children and the grandchildren can gain from the experience of the grandparents," Cathy Butler of the Seton Good Health School says, "whether they made mistakes and learned from them, or . . . were just heroic people, as many of them are."

But it is not just the families who need to hear these stories.

Few historians would dispute the argument that a valid retelling of the past must include not just the institutional record but also the stories of our ancestors' everyday lives. We have chronicles of wars, explorations, governments, inventions, and religions. What we lack is a clear record of daily domestic life: the food people ate, their clothing, the details of child rearing or caring for the sick and aged. We also lack a clear record of how people felt, how they responded emotionally to the daily challenges of their ordinary lives. For the most part, these records are missing because the cultural documents were written or compiled by men, who found little of interest or enduring value in domestic or emotional life. Historically, if women had learned to write and had been encouraged to write about their daily lives, it is likely that we would have a far greater understanding of how people of former cultures lived their lives.

Something of the same thing occurred in the earlier decades of the twentieth century. The women in the OWL Circle memoir workshops witnessed a massive transformation of private life, and women's evolving role in family, community, and work was one of its most conspicuous features. The personal stories of the women who experienced these changes make a direct, unmediated, and invaluable contribution to the history of ordinary life in our time. These stories also show us how ordinary private lives were impacted by the momentous events of a century marked by the extremes of humanity's creative and destructive potential. Later generations have only begun to adequately appreciate the character of women and men born before 1930 and forced by events to accept extraordinary responsibility at a very early age. These members of the "Greatest Generation" are dying, Tom Brokaw writes in his book based on their recollections (1998). If we neglect their stories now, they will be forever lost to history.

We have presented the memoirs in the nine chapters of *With Courage and Common Sense* much as the women wrote them, without significant editorial intervention. We corrected mistakes in spelling and grammar, changed an occasional sentence to make its meaning clear, and applied standard conventions of punctuation and capitalization. We also excerpted a few of the lengthier memoirs.

As they explored the ten workbook topics, most women wrote from six to eight memoirs, ranging in length from fewer than one hundred to several thousand words, and averaging around 250 words. Altogether, the forty-five OWL Circle workshops and their 455 writers produced some four thousand separate memoirs, around a million words, so the process of selection for this book required several iterations. In the selection process, we worked from the stories already collected in the workshop booklets, since the writers themselves judged them to be their "best" work. The memoirs we chose represent unique events, uniquely encountered and uniquely described, and yet typical of events in many women's lives. In that sense, each of these stories stands for the experience of countless other women, whose stories have gone—and will go—untold.

When we originally proposed the outline for this collection, we expected that the chapters would correspond to the topics from the OWL Circle workshops. But a slightly different pattern emerged from the memoirs themselves. We have used that pattern, because it obviously addresses significant themes in these women's lives.

Chapter One deals with the fundamental issue of identity and the formative experiences and cultural teachings that have engendered these women's sense of who they are. The memoirs in Chapter Two offer a strong sense of rootedness in the landscapes of home. Chapter Three presents stories about women's work life and the significant changes in their workplaces during their working lives. In Chapter Four, we have collected the family stories that teach family values and recall the sturdy but sometimes disturbing intimacies of parents, brothers and sisters, children and grandchildren, and extended family. Stories of romantic love and affectionate friendship appear in Chapter Five. The memoirs in Chapter Six reveal the many kinds of personal loss that women can encounter during a lifetime that spans six to nine decades—and the resilience and strong-heartedness that allows humans to live with and even learn from loss. Chapter Seven gives us a glimpse of the abundant fullness of women's experience, as they recollect large adventures and small ones, all personally significant. The stories in Chapter Eight recall decisive and often painful episodes in twentieth-century history from the point of view of ordinary women who were drawn willy-nilly into the extraordinary events of their time. Appropriately, the last chapter deals with legacies: with those physical things, those lessons, and those dreams that we inherit, shape, and reshape according to our experience, and then pass on to those who come after us.

Readers of these memoirs should judge them on their own terms, as the chronicles of small events that have grown large in the memories of their narrators, told plainly and without con-trivance, artifice, or striving for literary effect. One of the most delightful things about this collection, it seems to us, is that it captures the wonderfully authentic nuances of women's voices, spontaneous, unaffected, genuine, plain-spoken. Individually and in chorus, these women are memoirists first and writers after that, and their stories ring the truer because they have not been (as one OWL Circle participant put it tartly) "all gus-sied up."

As a collection, these stories offer a surprising glimpse into the astonishingly rich personal histories of the women who have told them, and who have every right to feel proud of all they have done and seen and experienced in their long lives. But in-stead of pride, what is most often sensed in these stories is a per-sonal modesty that does not boast of courage in hard times, but rather *shows* it—courage, yes, and common sense, that most serviceable if unfashionable virtue.

"Only connect," E. M. Forster wrote. Plain-spoken, coura-geous, heartfelt, these tales do just that. They connect their tellers with the remembered past of a century that has already gone. And they connect us, as hearers and readers, with the tellers, with their pasts and our own, and with the recognition that, at the bottom of it all, stories really do matter.

Susan Wittig Albert, Ph.D.

Dayna Finet, Ph.D.

NOTE

1. OWL Circle Project Teams
Management Team: Catherine Cogburn, Dayna Finet, Mary Jane Marks, Natalie Thomas.
Workbook/Facilitators' Manual Writing Team: Susan Wittig Albert, Catherine Cogburn, Dayna Finet, Sarah Gaetner, Joanne O'Neill.

BIBLIOGRAPHY

Women's life writing encompasses a wide range of forms: autobiography, memoir, journals, diaries, and letters. This bibliography offers a selection of items for readers interested in pursuing the topic of life writing by women, as well as complete listings for works cited in the Introduction.

Anderson, Linda. 1997. *Women and Autobiography in the Twentieth Century: Remembered Futures*. London and New York: Prentice-Hall/Harvester Wheatsheaf.

Anderson, Linda, and Trev Lynn Broughton, eds. 1997. *Women's Lives/Women's Times: New Essays on Auto/biography*. Albany: State University of New York Press.

Bateson, Mary Catherine. 1990. *Composing a Life*. New York: Plume Books.

Benstock, Shari. 1991. "The Female Self Engendered: Autobiographical Writing and Theories of Selfhood." *Women's Studies* 20: 5–14.

Benstock, Shari, ed. 1988. *The Private Self: Theory and Practice of Women's Autobiographical Writings*. Chapel Hill: University of North Carolina Press.

Birren, James E., and Donna Deutchman. 1991. *Guiding Autobiography Groups for Older Adults*. Baltimore: Johns Hopkins University Press.

Brokaw, Tom. 1998. *The Greatest Generation*. New York: Random House.

Brownley, Martine Watson, and Allison B. Kimmich, eds. 1999. *Women and Autobiography*. Wilmington, Del.: SR Books.

Conway, Jill Ker. 1998. *When Memory Speaks: Exploring the Art of Autobiography*. New York: Vintage.

DeSalvo, Louise. 1999. *Writing as a Way of Healing: How Telling Our Stories Transforms Our Lives*. New York: Harper Collins.

Heilbrun, Carolyn. 1988. *Writing a Woman's Life*. New York: Ballantine.

hooks, bell. 1999. *Remembered Rapture: The Writer at Work*. New York: Henry Holt.

Olsen, Tillie. 1978. *Silences*. New York: Delacorte Press.

Pennebaker, James. 1997. *Opening Up: The Healing Power of Expressing Emotions*. New York: Guilford Press.

Smith, Sidonie, and Julia Watson, eds. 1996. *Getting a Life: Everyday Uses of Autobiography*. Minneapolis: University of Minnesota Press.

———. 1998. *Women, Autobiography, Theory: A Reader*. Madison: University of Wisconsin Press.

Wagner-Martin, Linda. 1994. *Telling Women's Lives: The New Biography*. New Brunswick, N.J.: Rutgers University Press.

CHAPTER ONE

Identity

I Am Not Always the Same Person

A woman writing a memoir can begin almost anywhere. But many choose personal identity as a starting point. Perhaps it is easier to know who we have been in terms of who we are now.

To authentically know ourselves—past or present—is an immense challenge. Identity changes over time as a woman encounters the experiences that shape her evolving self, and self-recognition requires an often difficult, sometimes painful honesty that not everyone can achieve. The pursuit of authentic self-awareness requires a commitment of ongoing effort that some people cannot or will not make. But self-reflection can produce rich satisfactions, especially for women who by that process come to terms with their own growing and changing selves, and who come to acknowledge the integrity of their own brave and compassionate acts.

Women often see themselves primarily in the expectations of other people: parents, partners, children, even the anonymous stranger with an opinion about women's proper place. When the memoirs in this chapter and throughout the book address personal identity in terms of typical gendered roles in family and community, they tell us how women have found the significance of their lives in the context of the social world. And because we live not just for ourselves alone, but with others, these social roles have a valuable meaning.

But women memoirists, even those whose lives have been largely shaped by others' expectations, ultimately come to recognize through their writing their own unique and singular identities, made up not just of categories and roles but of an array of intellectual, emotional, and spiritual experiences that are exclusive to the self. They can say where and how they are unique, and where and what they share with others. In this chapter, we have gathered memoirs that purposefully, and sometimes painfully, explore identity.

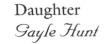

Daughter
Gayle Hunt

I am a daughter, and the oldest of four daughters. I was born in 1935 at home on the plains of West Texas during a terrible storm. The story goes that the doctor was summoned, and during the course of my delivery, the storm grew worse. Several tornadoes were sighted, so everyone decided to go to the storm cellar. But my mother refused to be moved, so I was born as the storm raged all around.

I was the first born, and a girl. A bitter disappointment. No girl names had been picked out, so I was not named for almost a month. My birth certificate just has Baby Girl Morris on it. Later, I was named Gale because I was born in a storm. The spelling was later changed to Gayle. I was never given a middle name.

I did not know this story until I was in my twenties, when my mother gave me my original birth certificate along with an amended birth certificate with my name on it. A couple of years ago I was at the Texas State Library, and I looked up my birth record in the genealogy collection.

I was still listed as Baby Girl Morris.

A Woman Named Billie
Billie Grace Herring

Throughout my life, I have struggled with the fact that I am female. Now, at sixty-six, I have finally come to terms with that fact.

I had an older (sixteen years) half sister, Hildegard, whose mother died when she was eleven years old. Our father remarried a couple of years later. When my mother and father decided to have a child, they were going to have a boy. He was to be named William (for my father) and Donald (for Mother's favorite doctor). As a contingency, Mother thought she would pick out a girl's name; she chose Grace Jeanette. But the assumption was that the baby would be a boy.

When I arrived female, I have been told, there was much consternation on the part of my parents. Daddy wanted a boy. Mother wanted a boy; she wanted to please him by having the son that his first wife had not.

Then there was the problem of a name. I am told that Daddy didn't like the name Mother had chosen but didn't have any clear alternative to suggest. After much discussion, Mother suggested Billie Grace. I was told endless times that my father's face brightened; he smiled and said he would like that very much because my name would at least be a derivative or diminutive of his name. So I became, at Mother's insistence, Billie-Grace. The hyphen was to ensure that I used both names and didn't drop Grace. The decision was also made to use the name Jeanette as a second middle name since my first name was Billie-Grace. To further confuse things, the doctor wrote the name incorrectly on my birth certificate—Janet, instead of Jeanette —so I became Billie-Grace Janet Ungerer.

Over the years, I experimented with being Billie or being Grace, but neither lasted a long time. I felt more comfortable as Billie-Grace and later dropped the hyphen, but never, never, never have I been Janet in any form. In fact, until recently, my grown sons did not know about that name. My husband Jim started calling me by my initials, BG, and now he and very close friends call me "BG."

✿ My Mother's Daughter
Katherine Koonce

I am my mother's daughter. As a small child, I'm sure I must have been a terrible nuisance, since I did not want to be very far away from my mother at any time. I have described myself as the original clinging vine. Often, people would say to me, "You look just like your mother." This was a puzzle to me, since my mother had very dark brown wavy hair and brown eyes and I had long blond braids and green eyes and freckles.

When I was five, I started kindergarten in Detroit, Michigan, at Parker Elementary. This was not a happy experience for me because Mother was at home where I wanted to be, and the kindergarten in my school was very strict. One day, I had to sit in the cloakroom because I was whispering at the wrong time. On another occasion, I started walking to school, then turned around and slipped in the side door of our house and hid there in a little alcove in the stairway. Of course, Mother heard me there and I got one of the few spankings of my life.

Naturally, I outgrew my childish clinging to my mother, but she always remained the rock in my life. Her wisdom, humor, and basic goodness helped me so many times in my life.

So now, if someone says "You remind me so much of your mother," I still may not know why, but I couldn't be prouder. There's no one I'd rather be like.

My Father's Daughter
Jo Scudder

My name is Ruby Jo, but I've always been called Jo. I think they wanted a boy. I am the middle of three girls, although I was raised in a lot of ways as a boy.

I was always with my father when he was not at work. I remember Saturday afternoons when I would go with him to town, to the grocery store and around. Always on Friday football nights I was at his side. My older sister was Mary Elizabeth after my two grandmothers, I was Ruby Jo after my mother, and my younger sister Howardene—after my father, of course.

I don't know if you can be affected while in the womb, but I sure liked boy things. When I was eight years old, I cried that Christmas because I didn't get a football suit, just a girl's bicycle. Always at recess at school and on the playground, I was the first one chosen for games, very athletic and competitive—and I still like sports. I married a boy who graduated with a degree in Physical Education. He planned to coach when he got out of the Army. As it turned out, he became a traveling salesman, but coached both our boys in playground sports. I still like boy things, am very comfortable with men, and at times I think like men.

I was not cut out to be a housewife. I really envy men the options they have to lead their own lives. Back when I was eighteen or nineteen, all girls could look forward to was being a housewife, teacher, nurse, or secretary. Thank goodness things changed as I got older. The last two years of my husband's stay at A&M we were married and I worked, just at Schaeffer's Book Store for fifty cents an hour, then at Bryan Air Force Base for better pay. Then my daughter was born, while we were stationed at Ft. Devens, Massachusetts. From then until 1981, I was a housewife and mother. With my last child in high school, I wised up and got a job—enjoyed every minute of it—wish I had had the sense to change before then.

❀ A Story about Who I Am
Ruby Johnston

I am a sister, a wife, a homemaker, and I was a church school worker. I come from a large family of twelve and over a hundred cousins.

My mother had twin sisters and no one could tell them apart, least of all their children. My mother was over ninety-eight years old when she died. A sister 104 years old died last year. She was a wonderful artist.

My father was a rancher. Our ranch came up to the edge of town. My sister was a nurse and looked after all the family, which sometimes created problems. She went to Chicago but didn't stay. Then she went to Arizona and worked in a hospital. I worked in Woolworth's and I knew everyone's name. You had to know everyone's name or they would not come to your counter.

I finished high school in Big Spring. I met my husband in the Depression years. We went to Dallas and married at my sister's church and returned to Big Spring, where two children were born. We lost our only son in a fall from a hill near town. Our daughter is an artist. She attended North Texas College. She taught twelfth-grade English for thirty years.

 ## All the Things I Am . . .
Williene Story

I am: a Christian widow, slow, a late bloomer, mother of two sons and two daughters, grandmother to eight, deaf, a sister, daughter of a one-hundred-year-old, a listener, encourager, correspondent, acknowledger of others' birthdays, friendly, patient, honest, loyal, perseverant, appreciative, strong, emotionally of few tears, mostly in control of temper, a church participant, and a collector of thimbles.

I have: blue eyes, graying brown hair, a five-foot six-inch heavy frame, bifocals, hearing aids, partial dentures, arthritic knees, and seventy-nine years of living.

I have been a: student, typist, interviewer, gift wrapper, cashier, recording secretary, family genealogist, shopper, traveler, teacher in college, high school, and primary special education, wife, lover, homemaker, keeper of children, seamstress, cook, house cleaner, laundress, chauffeur, guide, nurse, caregiver, yard worker, carpenter's helper, fruit picker, jelly maker, member of the Order of Eastern Star, musician (piano, bugle, clarinet, saxophone, voice), mover of hay, feeder of cows and dogs, tennis player, walker, skater, swimmer, biker, horseback rider, dancer, refinisher of furniture, painter of walls, and collector of autographs, souvenirs, baskets.

I enjoy: my family, reading, music (listening and doing),

flowers, full moon, swimming, creating, fireplace, knitting, red shoes, crochet, sweets, embroidery, antiques, needlepoint, family research, piecing quilts, receiving mail, painting, sightseeing, out-of-doors, color-stained glass, socializing with friends, and learning to use a computer.

I am proud of: a life of good experiences, earning a college degree, having family in Texas since 1834, guiding two sons to be Eagle Scouts and two daughters to equivalent ranks, having helped a good man acquire a home, and having helped a daughter with multiple sclerosis.

✿ I Am Not Always the Same Person
Marilyn Zimmerman

I am a child of God. I am a mature female, who is growing in a direction I like. I am fun-loving and I laugh a lot. I have a temper that I have learned to control, most of the time. I have been able to give up most of my judgmental ways and see the positives in the people that I meet. I have even learned to forgive myself, as I don't expect the perfection I once did, in others or myself. I am impatient. If I can't control a situation that needs to be handled, I can panic—for example, when the computer freezes, or the toilet overflows. Deep breathing has helped me to pause and rethink situations. I like to have things done immediately and waiting is a challenge. I am a good friend. If I sense someone's need, I will give up my own plans to do what I can to help. At times I can be too controlling in these situations, so I need to step back and reevaluate my motives. I'm getting better at this, perhaps because I have less energy.

I am a game player—games like bridge, party games, and golf. I like competition. I don't need to win, but I love the challenge, and of course winning is more fun than losing. I am a reader. I like to learn and am frustrated if I am unable to grasp a concept quickly. I enjoy being with people, but I need a fair amount of time by myself in order to function.

I enjoy my own company and am rarely at a loss for something to do. I like nature, being outdoors, and watching birds, butterflies, and insects. I like my garden, but don't like weeding for any length of time. I am not always the same person, so that if I wrote this tomorrow, there might be an entirely different version of me.

✿ Going to School
Oma Gillis

At the beginning of the fall school year after my sixth birthday, I started school in Grade One. Since both my parents were teachers or had been, I had been reading and writing for some time, and probably knew some basics of arithmetic. It was evident that I had mastered all that was taught in the first grade, so I was soon promoted to the second grade, completing both grades in my first school year. I also combined grades seven and eight in one year, so I was ready to enter high school at age twelve.

I was an avid reader during those years, and in the summer I made daily trips, either walking or roller skating, to the library to return the book I had read the day before and select another to take home. We walked to school. At noon, with an hour allowed, I also walked home for lunch. You had to walk rapidly at noon, but after school was out for the day, I probably dawdled along the way.

As I remember high school, everyone was required to take certain basic courses. You had a choice of electives to fill the day. I remember that one hour was called a study period. Latin was probably the most enlightening subject I took. With it, I finally clarified what I had been taught about English grammar. I recall once, when I was doing homework. Our assignment was to look through the dictionary and find ten new words not in our vocabulary and write sentences for each. In skimming the pages of the dictionary, I saw the word "piddle," which was defined as "to run slowly." I wrote the sentence "The little dog piddled down the middle of the road." After I had completed my ten sentences, my mother and father suggested I read them aloud. When I read the one about the little dog, they burst into gales of laughter and suggested that I probably should select another new word and write another sentence.

There were not a great many after-school activities for girls. There was a Home Economics Club. Both girls and boys could belong to the Debating Society, where we debated serious subjects, always beginning with "Resolved: That . . ." We had notes jotted down on index cards from which we spoke and on which we wrote comments for our rebuttal minutes. At home I took piano lessons and was supposed to practice an hour in the afternoon after school.

I graduated in 1923. All through my school years I had never received a grade below an "A." I began attending the University of Iowa the following fall. This was long before SAT tests were required or there were guidance counselors. Members of the incoming freshman class were required to take several hours of tests, however, at the time of registration. When these were graded, the best of the incoming students were assigned to professors who were to act as mentors, help in the selection of courses in the future, discuss problems, and generally assist in the choice of a major. I met with my assigned professor for about fifteen minutes, as I remember, and never saw or heard from him again.

I did find out that study of a second language was required, so before I graduated I had four years of French and two years of Spanish. I learned vocabulary, grammar, and read classics in these languages. There were no conversational classes, which would have been more valuable. Otherwise, I took courses that sounded interesting or were recommended by other students as having an interesting professor. Most of them were English courses, so I became an English major.

Before the start of my senior year, I was informed that I would need twelve hours of science to graduate. Most students took their science courses in their first and second years, but somehow I hadn't known about it. In my senior year, I took eight hours of chemistry and four hours of geology, and loved both courses. In fact, if I had taken chemistry as a freshman, I'm quite sure I would have continued with additional courses, and perhaps become a research chemist or something similar.

During my junior and senior years I was a "Reader" for one of the English professors. He had a large class in freshman English to whom he lectured. I read, corrected, and graded all the themes the students wrote. I suppose I was paid a nominal sum for this, but I don't remember.

My grades didn't always top the heap in those years. I still received an "A" in the majority of them, but if I didn't enjoy the course or found the subject matter uninteresting or dull, I would attend class and take notes and that was about all. I received a "B" usually in that case, and an occasional "C" crept in.

After graduating in 1927, I was still so young that my mother and father decided I should continue in the university to prepare further for a career in teaching. I came from a long line of educators, and since there were few careers open to women, it was assumed that I was a natural for becoming a teacher. So began a year when I learned to enjoy Chaucer in the original Middle English and read Beowulf in Old English. Fortunately, my guiding professor was the one with whom I had an excellent rapport and had read themes for, for two years. He advised me on the choice of a subject for my thesis and was one of the group that gave me the oral exams required to complete my master's degree.

So here was the finished product. I had just passed my twenty-first birthday. I had a Bachelor of Arts degree and a Master of Arts degree. I had the equivalent of seventeen years of education, condensed into fifteen. I was now five feet six and a half inches tall and weighed 105 pounds. I was an excellent dancer and could do the Charleston, the rage at that time. I played very good duplicate bridge, which was as far as bridge had evolved at the time. Actually, I knew practically nothing about anything in particular.

❧ A European Youth
Erika Eden

I am the matriarch of a wonderful large family. I have brothers; originally three, but I lost one. I have three sons and six daughters, and seven grandchildren ranging in age from twenty-one to nine years.

I've taught in elementary school as well as in community college. I was born in Germany and went to school in six different countries. My checkered education has stood me in good stead. I studied one year in France, three and a half years in Israel, one-half year each in Switzerland, Austria, and Holland.

I wrote a diary when I was about fourteen years old. It's about a series of events like vacations and trips. This diary reminds me of the many opportunities we had to see other places and meet other people and participate for a while in their lives, which were quite different from ours. On these trips we frequently lived with farmers in tiny villages of Austria, Switzerland, or France. We ate with them around their kitchen table, or helped them bake bread. No bread ever tasted as good as this freshly baked bread.

The reason for our many trips was the snobbish atmosphere around us in Berlin. My mother wanted to expose us to a simpler way of life. On one occasion we spent several months in a small Austrian mountain village. We went to school on skis. The school was a one-room schoolhouse. Every grade had one or two long benches. To assure the continuity of our lessons in Berlin, my mother hired a young man to teach us concepts we might miss, in math, history, or literature. The tutor also took us up some mountains, thus easing my mother's task of watching us all the time.

When I came to the U.S. in 1938 I ought to have attended high school, but my three younger brothers were in school. I went to work as a baby nurse. The small salary I made I shared with my family. Later, at nineteen, I tried to go to Hunter College. When they asked for my transcripts, I had none. But I said that I had studied the French Revolution in four countries in four different languages. I was accepted. I married a year later, and finally got my B.A. at SMU in Dallas—eight years and four children later.

✿ Girls Just Didn't Go to College
Gayle Hunt

The one burning desire that I have always had, ever since I could remember, was to go to college and get an education. But I graduated from high school in the early 1950s. Many of my girlfriends did go on to college and graduated, but in my family, girls just didn't go to college. There wasn't any money to send a girl to college. Besides, an education would just be wasted on a girl. I was encouraged to take a business course so I could get a job while waiting for some guy to marry me. Then I could work and put him through college.

I did marry and have children. But the dream never went away. I knew that someday I would return to the classroom.

We moved to Huntsville, Alabama, in 1966, and the University of Alabama campus was only a short distance from our home. My youngest child was in the second grade. What a wonderful opportunity! I could see the children off to school in the morning and arrange my classes so that I could be home when they got out of school. I did this for seven years, finally earning a degree in biology and chemistry.

Going back to school was the hardest thing I had ever done. I had to take some high school refresher courses before I could do the college work. Some of the professors were hostile to "older" women in the classroom (I was thirty-one years old at the time). My own family did nothing to help or encourage me. My mother was outraged that I could be so selfish.

My graduation was not a cause for celebration. My family didn't come. But that was okay. I had earned something that belonged to me. It's mine! And nobody can ever take it away. The self-satisfaction that it has given to me over the years is worth more than can ever be measured.

❀ A Lover of Back Roads
Martha Knies

I am a lover of back roads. Why take the fast lane when life is already going by too fast? I don't like traveling beside long semis and fast convertibles. Whizzing past fast-food franchises and outlet stores and overlighted automobile dealerships is not for me.

I like the slower lanes—not poky, mind you—just a little slower pace than the superinterstates. Sure, I get frustrated on curves and hills and even the straightaways, but then I tell myself that the slow driver could be my mother or father—or, God forbid, even myself a few years hence.

I like the surprises that back roads often bring: a creek, an old river bridge, lots of native trees and shrubs, cattle, sheep, goats, rock fences, old barns, cleared meadows, lovely country homes. I would like to have been the female version of Charles Kuralt—always on the road, meeting and talking with and writing about simple yet extraordinary folks along the way.

Yes, the back roads are for me, for around every curve or over the next hill, who knows what surprise might await?

Life is already moving by too fast, and as someone has said so well, life is a journey, not just a destination.

❀ Gifts That I Chose for Myself
Selah Rose

Starting over again in my sixties is the scariest thing I have ever done. It is right up there with the first day of school, the first act of love, first childbirth, and first position in a new career field. All those delicious feelings of anticipation and excitement posed with, in my case, sheer terror. Dread and desire wrapped up in the same gift box.

Gifts I chose for myself, highly valued and long awaited: knowledge, love, child rearing, career, independence, and yes, the starting over, freedom from the long tyranny of spousal abuse.

Yet each gift is purchased with a price, a cost to be counted, a sacrifice. Up until this point, each gift, each desire has been worth the price paid, I reason to myself. The cost of this freedom has been great: insecurity, financial loss, fear of the unknown future, uncertainty of direction, loss of role and purpose, lost identity, loss of approval of family and friends, loss of emotional support, loneliness, and deep grief.

The chosen gift is the opportunity to create a new life that fits my true self, my skills and abilities; fulfills my desires and needs; and expresses my own personality—the discovery of my real self, the one God created me to be.

Once again, thrills and terror merge in my soul, vex my thoughts, and paralyze my physical activity. Yet out of this numbness pulsates one tiny but powerful need: *to go for it!*

The divorce is three years past. The abusive forty-year marriage is history. The new little retirement abode is purchased. And, looking ahead, the best is yet to be.

Yeah, God willing, I am going for it.

CHAPTER TWO

Home
I Was Born
in East Texas

People need a place to belong. For as long as recorded history and probably before that, human consciousness has found protection, comfort, and stability in the ideal and the actual experience of home.

Home can mean a geographic place, and Texans especially identify with the peculiarly flamboyant identity of their home state. Generations of Texas women have enjoyed a reputation for remarkable spirit and substance. But women from other places, having adopted Texas through choice or necessity, always remember where they've come from, the regions or countries they have called home.

Home can also mean community, neighbors, and friends whose lives intersect for a time in meaningful ways, and when women write about the homes they remember, they also write about those with whom they shared those times and places. Home symbolizes the universal human dynamic of stability and change, remembering the past and planning for the future, going back and moving on.

For women, the mention of home inevitably invokes the domestic setting, the remembered look and feel of childhood homes and the homes they have made for families of their own. While these memories are often pleasant and satisfying, women can also be reminded of the burdens of home work, of the

35

cooking, cleaning, and caretaking that have kept them so continually occupied. As twentieth-century progress has revolutionized domestic technology, expectations about homemaking and the tools for doing it have changed radically. As late as the middle of the century, a rural Texas home might have had no indoor plumbing, no electricity, and no phone. Women grew vegetables and fruits at home, then harvested and preserved them. Women raised livestock at home, then did the work of slaughtering and cleaning. Women milked cows and cleaned out stable muck. Few women now cope with such intense domestic tasks. But at century's end, they still do most of the housework and labor longer hours than ever before.

In this chapter, women recall their homes, sometimes nostalgically, sometimes with wry humor, sometimes with a fierce pride in the accomplishments of mothers and grandmothers who made do with what they had. Houses may indeed vanish, but these homes have endured in the memories of the women who made them.

I Was Born in East Texas . . .
Helen G. Burton

I was born in East Texas in Henderson County, at the farm-house of my grandparents. My parents were delighted with the new arrival and quite put off by the famous remark of my grand-father, Benjamin Greer, upon first viewing the new baby: "She's a little bit dish-faced, isn't she?"

My childhood home was made of wood, painted white, with one story. It was next to the Methodist Church, which would have been convenient to walk to Sunday school, but we were Baptists and our church was on the other side of town. I joined the Baptist Church in Elkhart, Texas, at age seven. I do recall that the minister walked down the aisle and held my hand and asked the critical questions, such as "Do you love Jesus?" and received the appropriate responses. I walked to the front of the church for the audience to file by and shake my hand.

We had a detached garage with a small room attached where our maid lived. Her name was Louise Giles, and her favorite ex-pression was, "Ah ain't studyin' you, chile!" At this time, there were six children in our family, plus a teenager who lived with us. Though my parents were not overly superstitious, the col-ored maids kept us informed about dangers such as "The boo-german is gonna get you, chile, if you don't do so-and-so." We were afraid of the boogeyman, and afraid of God, too, asking forgiveness in our nightly prayers.

We thought nothing of sleeping three in a bed—we always did. We would gather beside Dad and Mother in bed at night because our father read fairy tales to the youngest children, and all of us listened. My father always made the appropriate animal noises that the narrative suggested.

We always ate together and went home from school every day for lunch. The bus students brought their lunch, because there were no school cafeterias then. I was always envious of the kids who got to bring their lunch from home. Their bologna sand-wiches wrapped in newspaper seemed much more desirable than our hot biscuits and fried chicken. Sometimes I would get my girlfriend to share her lunch with me at recess and I would take her home with me to have lunch. Mother always welcomed a "little guest." Dad always sat at the head of the table, and Mother was the cook and waitress. We often had a "bottle washer" in the kitchen. We said grace before every meal, and my father always said it.

We were poor, but did not know it. My father handled the money, but Mother had charge accounts and he had a regular paycheck. Mother would sometimes let us charge at the drugstore and the dry goods store. Dad would yell when the bills came in. Mother made our clothes and mopped the floors at night after we had all gone to bed (the only time she could keep us from tracking it up, she said).

We had gas heat in that house, and I was standing in front of the radiant-type heater one morning, wearing a white outing nightgown (my "angel costume") when it caught fire. I ran out of the front door and my Aunt Winnie followed. My father was in the bathtub and my mother was out in the back checking on Louise, who was ill. The subsequent severe burns I received before my father put the fire out kept me bedridden for six months, and the family doctor ministered to me at home. I missed almost a year of school, and to this day I shudder when I think of this ordeal in the days before miracle drugs and hospital burn units. I was promoted to the next grade, but was forever the smallest, most immature girl in my class, graduating from high school at age fifteen.

We later moved to a larger house where we had a side yard for playing croquet and baseball. Roses and wisteria bloomed in the yard. By this time, there were nine children in our family—I was the second. My father was the school superintendent and a state senator, and a big supporter of Franklin Roosevelt. Because of this, we had a lot of visitors—schoolteachers and people looking for WPA [Works Progress Administration] jobs during the Depression. I remember my mother giving bowls of soup or oatmeal to vagrants who passed through on the train. People came and went at our house, and my dad was always in a "helping mode." He wrote letters to Washington to get people on the WPA and young men into the CCC [Civilian Conservation Corps] camps.

There were no jobs except under government programs. They started a canning program at our school, and unemployed women were paid to can the surplus meats and vegetables supplied by the local farmers. There was no market for their produce because people had no money. Growers would throw their produce into the ditches. My dad was a stoic, and he always kept an optimistic attitude. He believed in putting people to work and believed the jobs program was sound. We always had a Victory Garden for our family, which my father tended.

I don't remember the number, but we had a telephone and we called the operator "Central." We sometimes called the operator and asked her to give us the time of day in Chicago. She was always angry with us and reported us to our father. We only had one telephone.

My entire family enjoyed music as we were growing up. We had a piano and certain selected sisters were given piano lessons. Maureen would play the piano and we would all sing together: church songs, folk ballads, old favorites like "I Dream of Jeannie with the Light Brown Hair" and "Annie Laurie." My father taught us to sing some of the old ballads he knew from his father, growing up. We listened to the radio as a group when special programs were on, and all of us read a lot of books. We didn't have many pets, but I remember a dog my brother named Snowball. He was a cur, but much loved by the family. He loved to chase cars and I think he was finally killed by one.

Growing up, we looked forward to the short trips (though they seemed long at the time) to our grandparents' farm at Christmas and in the summers. Aunt Lizzie, our maiden aunt, lived with her parents and always had a supply of teacakes (molasses cookies) and baked sweet potatoes awaiting us. We also had farm-grown peanuts and popcorn, made into popcorn balls.

I was married to Horace Burton, a sailor, on December 19, 1944, at the University Baptist Church in Austin, Texas, and remained his partner until his death April 4, 1993, on the cruise ship *Stella Solaris* during a Panama Canal crossing. Our three children are Lucy Greer Burton, born in 1947; Douglas Gray Burton, born in 1951; and George Palmer Burton, born in 1962, and we have three grandchildren. When I got married, my father came to give me away, but my mother stayed at home with the rest of the brood. My husband always adored my mother. He couldn't imagine how she coped with a household of nine children, a husband, and visitors, but she managed, and kept a sense of humor about it all.

❁ How My Mother Got Her Washing Machine, and Other Stories
Janie Kirkpatrick

A farm is a great place for a child to grow up. There are so many interesting things happening and there is so much space to explore. We lived seventeen miles from the nearest town, which only had about 10,000 people. We had a small community about five miles from us. There was a school, a church, and a small grocery store.

My parents had moved to New Mexico from Oklahoma in 1929. My mother used to say that she had two families. She had four children born in Oklahoma, in the space of seven years. Then she waited six more years before I was born, the first of her children to be born in New Mexico. Two more came after me. My younger sister was born five years after me; my younger brother came three years later. I imagine that the last three of us were a big surprise. Birth control was not too effective in those days.

The original owners of the house my parents bought in New Mexico had built a two-room house to live in while the larger house was being built. We used one room of the smaller house for a laundry room. We also hung meat in it to cure. The other room was used at times as a brooder room for chickens. At other times, it served as a bedroom for a hired hand. When asking the location of an item, the answer would often be, "It's down the old house." Eventually, the smaller house came to be referred to as "down the old house."

Our house had no electricity or bathroom plumbing in my early years. We did have running water in the house, but no hot-water heater. The house had two bedrooms and the older boys slept in a basement where we also kept the coal that fueled the furnace that heated the whole house. In the winter, Mom would bring in the tubs and put them close to the fire, heat water, and we would bathe in the living room by the furnace. My brothers always had to leave when I was being bathed. When the weather was warmer, we would bathe in the room set aside as the bathroom.

My mother had her hands full cooking and caring for her growing family. She also had the responsibilities of a farm, such as caring for chickens, growing a garden, canning, feeding the pigs, and helping when animals were butchered for food. Laundry was a big problem, and when I was born she thought it was time that they acquired a washing machine to make her life a little easier. My father was never one to spend money on things that couldn't be used to make money, so a washing machine wasn't too important to him. My mother told the story of how she got her washing machine.

Washing was quite an ordeal. The laundry room had an old cast-iron pot that had to be filled with water. Then a fire was built underneath to heat the water. Tubs had to be placed on wooden tables and were filled with hot water from the big pot. This had to be done with buckets as there was no pipe to the large pot. Then the clothes had to be washed on a rub board and rinsed in the tubs. Dirty water had to be dumped out and replaced. In the summer, the room became very hot. Clothes had to be wrung out by hand and hung on the line to dry.

On this particular day, Mother had decided that she just had to have some help with the laundry. So when my father came by the door of the "down the old house," she told him that he would just have to help her. But he replied that he had to go see a neighbor about a tractor and maybe if he got back in time, he'd help her. This made her very angry, and when he left, she told herself that if she could stay as mad as she was at that moment until he came back, she would get herself a washing machine. So she talked to herself while she did her laundry. She told herself that she deserved better, that she had worked hard and not complained but that it was too much to have to take care of a new baby and do all the other things she had to do and not have any help.

By the time my father came back, Mother was madder than she had been when he left. She let him have it. I think that the main thing that got my father was when she told him that if she kept working so hard, she might die, and then he would be left to take care of the kids. My father knew when he was beaten, and he said he reckoned that they could go the next day and get her a washing machine. Of course, it was not an automatic. It was the old wringer type with some kind of engine (I thought gasoline, but I'm not sure because of the fire in the room). But it was a lot better than washing on a rub board or by hand. I can remember getting my hand caught in the wringer and being really scared. But my mom calmly turned the wringer the other way, and my arm went back through.

I had three older brothers and one sister, but no other children around to play with. The older brother closest to my age was six years older. I remember entertaining myself a great deal. I used my imagination and was Jane (as in Tarzan and Jane) as I climbed trees. I played on the tractors when they weren't being used. I was allowed to ride horses at an early age but only when someone was around to keep an eye on me. I had kittens and cats that my mother fed scraps from the table. We always had dogs around, but I never paid much attention to them. In the summer I was allowed to paddle around in the stock tank from which the cattle drank, if Daddy had cleaned it recently. I shudder at that now, but I never was sick from getting in that water. I explored the pasture east of the house and walked over the cattle guard. I walked the fences in the stock pens and filled the barrels that were empty.

We had a very large chicken house and a smaller one that was occasionally used for a brooder house. It had wire strung across the front, and the wire became the front window of my little playhouse. I would clean it up and scrounge around for boxes for tables and large rocks for chairs for my little house. I would use old tin cans and do pretend cooking. My mother invaded my little house one day and put a stop to my use of an old gallon bucket as a potty. We did not have a bathroom in the house until I was ten years old. We had an outhouse and a catalog. My parents had what they called a slop jar in their bedroom (it had a lid) and I guess I used it occasionally at night, if it was raining outside. So, I had incorporated the gallon can as my slop jar in my little play house.

Hired hands were an interesting part of farm life. My father would hire them from the employment office in town. They would work for a season and then be gone. Daddy had a way of getting rid of them when he was through with them. Rather than just telling them he had no more work for them, he would have them clean out the stock pens. That was a rather nasty job and they would decide there were other ways to earn money and they would quit. I mentioned that sometimes one room of the "down the old house" would be used to house the hired help. But if the hired hand had a wife or family, they would live in a boxcar that was located northwest of the house and barns, next to a field. There was no plumbing or electricity in it. I remember my uncle and aunt lived in it for a short time, and they had it fixed up so it was quite livable.

My dad hired a man and helped him move his wife and baby into the boxcar. One Sunday night about a week after they had moved in, I was home by myself while the family went to church. Someone knocked on our front door. Today, this seems a little scary, but we had no fear that anything would happen to us in those days. We had no locks on the doors. So I answered the door and a lady was standing there. She asked if I knew a certain man. I said that I did, that he and his wife were living in our boxcar and he was working for us. She replied that the woman with him wasn't his wife, that she was his wife, and that she had contacted the sheriff to find him and that the lady would have to leave. The next day, Daddy helped the first lady move back to town with her baby, and the original wife (I guess) moved in with her daughter. The man continued to work for us for about nine months.

We grew wheat, and harvesting it was a big undertaking. Daddy would contract with someone who had a harvesting machine and they would work long hours getting it in before it rained or hailed. Timing was important. We cooked big noon dinners for the hands, and often carried box lunches to them in the fields in the late afternoons so they could continue working as late as possible. Sometimes, I would get to ride in the harvesting machine bins (if there was someone to watch me, for it was very dangerous). Sometimes, I would get to ride in the truck to town, where we sold the grain. This was fun for me as we would often stop and get a Coke.

I was a tomboy in that I would rather play the cowboys and Indian games with the boys than play house with the girls. I didn't know the name of any cowgirls so I was trying to think of something to call myself that sounded Western. I came up with Mae West. That sounded pretty Western to me.

   Keeping House for My Mother
Betty Martin

I guess I grew up poor, but I didn't know it until I was nearly grown. Sure, some of the people in my neighborhood had nicer homes and furniture, but I didn't really think about it then. It just seemed to me that everyone I knew had to pinch pennies. My mother worked to support herself and me from the time I was five years old, and I became our housekeeper. Mother and I shared a house with another family of six. The mother of the other family took care of me and fed me the six days that my mother worked.

I was proud of our two rooms and a back porch. My mother and I shared one room as a bedroom, and the other room became our living room. The other family had to walk through our kitchen (it was really a porch) to reach the one bathroom in the house. I usually had my meals with the other family. On Sundays, when my mother and I were sitting in our kitchen eating the one weekly meal that we could have together, there was always a parade of people heading for the bathroom. I just thought everybody lived that way.

I don't remember when I started making up the bed and picking up after my mother and me, but I took pride in doing it, believing that I was really a big help to my mother. Some helper! I pulled the sheet and spread up and the bed was made, and then I just moved the dust around on end tables and dresser tops. It didn't even occur to me to lift the objects or dust the sides of furniture. Only the tops mattered. By the time I was ten, I was doing laundry for my mother and myself, washing our clothes by hand in the bathtub and even making a stab at ironing them. If my mother touched up her blouses before wearing them to work, I didn't know it.

Before I married at eighteen, I was still washing clothes in the bathtub, but that method soon ended. My husband Jack came from a different lifestyle. He introduced me to the Laundromat! We were both still very young, so of course we would put off the washing chore until all of our clothes were soiled. Then we would bundle everything up, ride the city bus to the Laundromat, and bring the wet laundry home to hang it while it dried. One weekend, we hung all my new gifts of bridal lingerie on the line, left them to dry while we went to a movie, and returned home to find that all of them had been stolen. To this day, I have never been extravagant enough to buy that fancy kind of stuff for myself. I guess you might say that I'm more the practical sort.

I do not think I was harmed by attempting to do adults' work so early in life. From my first job of keeping house as a child, I learned to be a pretty good housekeeper and still take pride in a nice clean home. I even learned to move objects when I dust, and modern technology has eliminated the bathtub washing and the risk of clothes disappearing when left on a line to dry.

Courage and Little Else
Helen Ibbotson

I was born in 1927. My early years were spent in a rural setting with no household conveniences. It was the beginning of the Depression and due to my father's alcoholism, he had lost a very good position with Conoco Oil Company and failed to be sober long enough to hold another. When I was nine, my mother, with great courage and little else, moved us to Commerce, Texas. She was able to rent a house and rent out rooms to college students. Mother was a nurse but had no job at first, and things were very uncertain. I had one sister, but the daughter of some close friends moved to Commerce with us and shared a room with Bobbie and me. Her name was Georgia, and she is like my other sister—in fact, I am closer to her than my real sister. Georgia's parents, who were prosperous farmers, often drove down and brought us food.

Chores, Chores, Endless Chores
Mary Lou Morgette

Chores, chores, endless chores. I can't remember when we weren't expected to help out with work around the house, and later, in the fields. We always had chickens, and even little ones can gather eggs. Usually the eggs were just lying there in the nest and were easy picking. But sometimes a hen was on the nest and she did not care to give up her eggs. Her maternal instincts took over and she expected chicks to appear if she sat long enough— so she did not want to move over. She also did not want you to reach under her to take the eggs. It was a challenge. Sometimes she would flog you, that is, spread her winds and fiercely chase you. But I had been sent to gather eggs and I did not want to go to the house empty-handed.

One of the dreaded chores to do with chickens was to clean out the hen house. This meant you replaced the straw in the nests, then you raked the pen, under the roosts and in the chicken yard. Cleaning out chicken droppings is not a pleasant job. The chickens were a source of food, as in eggs and meat, and of feathers for pillows, so they weren't all bad. However, it was not a lot of fun to catch a chicken, wring its neck, put it into hot water and then pick off all the feathers. This was necessary if we wanted to have fried chicken, which we did often.

Besides chickens we had cows, one when we lived in town and more when we were on the farm. As soon as I could be trusted with the bucket of milk and handling the cow, I learned to milk. You always put feed in the trough to keep her busy while you did your work. You also put hobbles on her back legs so she didn't kick over your bucket of milk. That was a definite no-no. Not only did you lose your milk, but also you were in for a severe scolding. That milk was for the family to use, and it was not to be wasted by carelessness. Anyway, before you began to milk the cow, you first had to wash her udder. In winter you used warm water. I guess you wanted to butter her up! Then you sat on your little stool and squeezed and pulled until there was no more milk. Once you were finished you set the cow free and headed to the house with your milk.

If we had only one cow, the milk was strained into crocks and set in the refrigerator. After several hours the cream rose to the top. Mother would take most of this heavy rich layer off for making butter or sometimes for whipping. The milk that was left was still rich, so we really didn't have skim milk. I didn't like that anyway. I liked rich milk and drank plenty of it, so it's no wonder I got fat! The milk we used was not homogenized or pasteurized, but Daddy was careful to keep the cows healthy, so we never had any health problems from it.

When we lived on the farm we usually had at least five cows

and sometimes more. That meant everyone had more than one cow to milk. Cows must be milked in the morning and in the evening, so we all developed our squeezing muscles. The milk was put through a separator, which separated the cream from the milk. You strained the milk into a bowl on top. As you turned the handle, the cream came out of one spout and the milk came out of the other. These were put into separate cans and taken to town to sell.

We kept some of the cream to make butter and also sold it. There were two kinds of churns, and we used both at one time or another. My favorite—the one I minded least—was the crock with the dash coming up through a hole in the lid. The dash was a stick with four spokes, to churn the cream on the bottom. This churn sat on the floor so you could sit or stand as you raised and lowered the dash until the butter was formed. When there was a ball of butter you knew you had beat all the butter out of the cream. This could take a while, so it was good to change positions. The Dazey churn was a big glass jar fitted with a lid that had beaters and a turn wheel. While the dash churn could be monotonous, the Dazey churn was an accident waiting to happen. I liked to turn it fast, and more than once the jar slid across the cabinet or almost fell to the floor. I'm sure it did as good a job as the floor model, but I never really appreciated it. Mother took the ball of butter out of the churn, salted it, and patted it between her hands to remove all the milk. Then she put it into a rectangular wooden mold, which held one pound of butter. She sold any we did not need.

Another source of food was the garden. Mother always had a variety of vegetables, from beans, peas, and tomatoes to okra, squash, corn, onions, beets, and cucumbers. All of us were expected to help in planting, weeding, watering, and gathering things in the garden. One vivid, early memory of gardening responsibilities was about a time we lived in town but Mother and Daddy went to work at the farm. They left Paul, Wanda, and me at home. Part of the chores we were left to do was to plant some beans. We played a long time and then decided Mother and Daddy would soon be home so we got busy with

our bean planting. We made quick work of it and happily reported how we had done what we were told. Several days later,
bean sprouts began to appear—all in one spot. We had been in
such a hurry to get our planting done that we just dumped all
the seeds in a heap without realizing how they would come
up. I learned a lesson that day, as well as getting a whipping.
Mother's words rang in our ears a long time as she told us: "Be
sure your sins will find you out." I may have tried to cover up
other rebellions, but I never planted beans like that again.

We had another memorable garden disaster, in similar circumstances. Mother and Daddy had gone to the farm, leaving
the young ones at home. We played quite a while before we
were bored with what we had been doing. We spotted a cotton
sack—a six-foot-long canvas sack with a shoulder strap. We decided we could give each other rides. One of us would sit on the
end of the sack and another one would put the strap over the
shoulder and pull. I'm not sure how we chose our racetrack,
but it turned out to be the garden. This was not a newly planted
garden or a garden that had been harvested. This garden was at
its prime. When Mother saw what we had done she was not a
happy woman, and that is an understatement. The full weight
of her wrath fell on us that day.

We girls learned to cook well before we got to Home Ec
classes. Biscuits were one of my first lessons. We knew we were
part of the preparation, serving, and cleanup crew.

Ironing was another of our regular chores. You need to understand several things. There were no permanent-finish fabrics
or synthetics. Everything was cotton, some rayon and silk. The
rayon wrinkled a lot when it was washed and needed a cool iron
unless you wanted to burn a hole in it. The cotton wrinkled a lot
too, and most of the clothes were starched. They were washed,
dipped in heavy starch (boiled, not spray starch), and hung outside on the line to dry (no gas dryers). When they had dried they
were sprinkled with water to dampen them, so you might have
a hope of getting the wrinkles out. You wrapped them into a
bundle to allow the dampness to be distributed. I am not sure
why you dried them in the first place if you were only going

to get them wet again. Anyway, your clothes were ready to be ironed. Before we had an electric iron we used flat irons. These were heavy cast iron, sort of wedge-shaped. You needed two of these because they had to be heated on a burner of the stove, then picked up with a handle that fitted over the wedge. The iron was usually very hot when you first took it off the stove. As you ironed, it got cold, and then you left it to heat and picked up the other one. One thing you learned early was to never put the hot iron down in the middle of a garment until you knew it was not so hot. If you did there was a brown wedge-shaped spot on that garment and it had to be washed again, or at least put in the sun, with hopes of getting the scorch out. The heavy-duty starch, about the consistency of wallpaper paste, made scorching a regular occurrence. If we wanted to press a wool garment, we covered it with brown paper, which we wet, then ironed that paper. Now every time I iron I appreciate a good steam iron and a can of spray starch.

❀ A Lesson for Young Brides
Oleta Cates

It took a long time for me to please my husband with my cooking. It was a daily chore, and over the years I learned a few secrets I'd like to pass on.

My husband was a gourmand, and I was expected to be a gourmet cook from Day One because his first wife was one and his mother was one. The first secret I learned was how to make like-to-die-for homemade dinner rolls.

My three children were in grade school and since it was a small new school, I spent lots of time there working at PTA projects and helping in the office and lunchroom. The first time I had lunch in the lunchroom I couldn't believe the rolls! I asked the cook for her recipe. (This was before the day of frozen rolls or frozen dough.) She told me they ordered them weekly. They came frozen in packages of ten dozen. I asked her to please get me a package, which she did. I hid them in the bottom of my deep freeze and brought them out a dozen at a time, let them rise, and served them hot. It was assumed that I whipped them up myself and I certainly didn't enlighten anyone. The first time I served them at a dinner party one of my guests asked for the recipe. I got out my best cookbook, wrote the recipe down and gave it to her.

The next lesson I learned was easy. I believe that any food tastes better if you can smell it as you come in the door. So if I had a busy day and I didn't get home early enough to prepare a great meal, I fried a big pan of onions and served hamburgers with all the fixings. The onion smell did the trick every time.

My best secret was how to cook roast beef to please everyone. One son liked his beef well done, two sons and I liked ours medium, and my husband preferred (or demanded) that the roast be bloody rare. Unless I bought at least a ten-pound roast it was impossible to have it cooked all three ways. When I finally learned the secret, I had done a standing rib roast but forgot to check the thermometer, so it was too well done.

Something told me to slice the roast before I took it to the table. I reached for the red food coloring and soaked the center slices. My husband said, "You finally learned to cook a roast just the way I like it."

Don't ever believe that red dye in food coloring will kill you. I did this for twenty years and used gallons of the stuff.

✿ Horses, Friends, and Cleaning Out the Stalls
Sarah McKinney

As a state employee, my husband had been transferred to Paris, Texas, in that wonderful northeastern part of the state. (It was our third transfer in four years.) Knowing our stay would most likely be temporary, we decided it would be wisest to rent a home until or if we found we would be staying in Paris for any length of time. We did find a nice, modest little brick house, with two bedrooms, one bath, kitchen, breakfast room, dining room, and living room. It was perfect for our needs.

As soon as the moving van pulled away from our new home, the front doorbell rang and I opened the door. On the porch stood two young girls who appeared to be just about the age of our son Sam, who was twelve years old at the time. One was obviously the older sister, and she held out a plate of cookies to me, welcoming us into the neighborhood, while the other girl held a basketball cradled in the crook of her arm. Both girls were smiling broadly and had their blond hair rolled on huge pink rollers.

After handing the plate of cookies to me, the older girl introduced herself and her little sister as Paula and Billie Ausmus. Her next words were, "Can your little boy come out and play with us?"

Thus began a friendship that developed into a great love for these girls which lasts to this day. It would be impossible to pick out any one occasion that was the happiest because there were so many wonderful times shared with "our girls next door."

Paris and the surrounding area were rich agricultural and ranching communities. We soon found ourselves joining the "horsey" set and justified buying our first horse by saying it would be for Sam. The first horse was soon joined by a second horse and then a third, so all three of us had a horse. Before long, Paula and Billie were given a horse by their mother and, of course, this horse was kept with ours. We had rented a fifty-acre pasture of beautiful green rolling hills, with plentiful grass for grazing and several copses of shade trees. There was even a picturesque tank, a pond which provided drinking water for the horses while they were out in the pasture. The rented pasture included a Yankee-style barn with stalls for the horses, a feed room for storing barrels of oats, a hay loft, and a tack room. Mac built a saddle tree for each of us to keep our saddles and blankets on, and each of us had our own special places for hanging bridles, halters, and tie-downs.

One of my fondest memories is of wintertime stall cleaning.

During severe cold weather, we kept the horses in their individual stalls, going out each morning and each evening to check on them and feed and water them. On weekends, the three of us plus the two girls had a standing obligation to go out to the barn for stall cleaning. We were usually joined by two other families who had decided to keep their horses with ours and shared in the cost of the barn and pasture, so it was really party time for all. We kept an electric hot plate in the tack room, so there was always a pot of fresh, hot coffee on those cold winter days, and the young people were considered old enough to drink coffee to help stay warm.

Each of us cleaned out the stall of our own horse. Raking out the old hay and putting it into wheelbarrows and carting it out to the barnyard for burning was pure and simple pleasure. It could have been an unpleasant and dreaded chore. However, when mixed with constant giggles and stifled screams from the younger ones, pleasant conversation and shared laughter from the older ones, it brought all of us together in our mutual desire to care for our beloved steeds.

Does one have to be crazy to say that cleaning out horse stalls was one of the happiest times of one's life? Maybe so. But I like being crazy.

Aunt Hattie's House
Janice Wilkins

Aunt Hattie was my grandmother's sister. She was a surrogate grandmother to my sister and me. We had never lived near my grandmother, and she died before I ever really got to know her. After my father died, we moved into the house where Mother had grown up. Aunt Hattie lived down the road from us. Our little family was included in all of her family get-togethers during the holidays.

She was a special lady. After her husband killed himself, she stayed on the farm and raised five children by herself. When we moved into the old house down the road from her, the children were all grown and gone, and she still lived on the farm, raising chickens, cattle, and some crops.

What I remember most fondly about my visits to her house were her teacakes. She always had a plate of the *best* teacakes under the cup-towel on the dining table. It was the custom to leave the salt, pepper, sugar, etc., on the table at all times covered with a cup-towel between mealtimes. As a child, whenever I would walk by the table, I could reach under the cloth and come out with a treat. I wonder if one of those teacakes would taste as good if I had it now, or if they were so tasty because sweet treats were so few and far between.

Since Aunt Hattie took care of the cattle and chickens by herself, the animals were not used to being around men. When my uncle came to help worm and dehorn the cattle, the cattle became alarmed by his presence, jumped the fence, and ran off into the pasture. He had to return to the house while Aunt Hattie went to coax the cattle back to the pen.

For all her hard work and life situations, the only worry that I ever heard her express was the concern that one day hay might be stored in her house. It is a common practice in rural areas of Central Texas for hay to be stored in old deserted houses. When I returned to the area for Mother's funeral four years ago, I drove by to visit the area where I had grown up. Aunt Hattie would be happy to know that a family, not hay, occupied her house.

❀ Finding Home
Grace B. Schmitt

We were a moving kind of family, so I have snatches of memories from different parts of New York. I was born in Manhattan and lived there until I was about eight years old. For some of those years, I don't know how many, we lived in an area called Greenwich Village, down near the tip of Manhattan. We lived in an apartment, I guess a tenement, on about the third floor, and a girl I played with all the time lived across the street. Her apartment had a gate and a small courtyard in the center with a turtle pond. We both loved that turtle and spent hours playing with it. Also across the street was the Greenwich Village Playhouse where my sister Helen was active in the Little Theater groups. Mom was forever sewing costumes for her, and Helen was so glamorous in her long skirts and feather boas. Mom made me a very twirly skirt one time, and I loved to spin around and watch it swing out. I think Mom wore herself out sewing for Helen, because sometime in my teens she taught me how to sew, and I made a lot of my own clothes after that.

Several years ago when Karl and I were back east we decided to show our son Mike and his daughter Stephie the Big Apple. I decided that Greenwich Village was a good place to go. We wandered around a while, but nothing looked familiar until we came to Barrow Street and it sent off bells in my memory. We turned down the street and soon we noticed that a number of buildings had been torn down, leaving half a block empty. There was just one apartment left standing at the other end of the street. Just then, a man with his dry cleaning slung over his shoulder passed us and stopped ahead to get his keys out. He opened a gate, and suddenly I knew that was my friend's apartment. Beyond the gate I could see a garden and a courtyard. I asked him if there was a turtle pond there. He said no, but invited us in for a look. I declined, because I felt sure that the one remaining apartment house, across the street, was my family's. We crossed the street to look at it and I turned around to look back at my friend's apartment. As I did so, there, just a little further down the street, was the Greenwich Village Playhouse, still doing the many different programs it was doing all those years ago.

CHAPTER THREE

Work

Making Something
That Lasted

Long before late-twentieth-century American feminism, women by the millions worked outside their homes. For these women, the meaning and the value of work has varied as much as the conditions of work. Women's participation in the paid labor force has represented a necessary, often indispensable, contribution to their families' survival. Through paid employment, they have created the economic foundation for their own autonomy. In work, women have found their calling and won an otherwise unobtainable personal and professional fulfillment.

Women who came of age in this century have worked at an impressive variety of jobs. Some of these required long and arduous physical labor, usually with low pay and no opportunity for improvement or growth. In jobs now considered traditionally female, like teaching and nursing, they performed essential work for compensation far beneath its value. And in nontraditional fields, particularly in the professions, they labored against unfair constraints to succeed in mostly male domains. Women's stories about the challenges, obstacles, satisfactions, and rewards of their work in the middle of the century and before are especially important to us now. We have more opportunities, and it is easy to forget how our grandmothers and mothers struggled to find work worth doing.

As the OWL Circle women began to write about their work,

it was clear that the work they valued most was work that created "something that lasted," as Kathryn Doggett puts it in the title memoir of this chapter. They valued not just handwork, but work that required them to use their minds and their hearts, and they still recall with delight the satisfactions of making their own way and of making a contribution to the community and the nation, particularly in a time of war.

Although none of this came easily, women have gained increasing success at the business of "making something that lasts." But we are also reminded in these essays that our work can also be our craft and our art, performed with love, with head and hands and, yes, with heart.

And in the end, it is the heart that lasts.

Making Something That Lasted
Kathryn Doggett

When I was ten years old, my mother gave me two choices. I could learn to sew and make my brothers' shirts and my own clothes, or I could stay in the kitchen with her and cook. I chose sewing because I preferred making something that lasted, and wasn't just gobbled up by my four older brothers.

Mother patiently taught me how to lay out a pattern, using knives to weight the flimsy pattern paper on the brightly colored feed sacks, then how to use the Singer treadle machine. I enjoyed sewing and continued making nearly all my clothes.

I can remember making our daughter's little dresses as she sat beside or on the sewing machine and watched. Since Bill and I were struggling with finances, as all our young married friends were, I could not afford to buy new material for Donna's clothes. I would go to the Humane Society's rummage store in Austin and buy a full-gathered print skirt that had about three or four yards of material, rip it apart, and then make the dresses. One of the cutest coats she ever had when she was about four was one I cut from a lady's coat that even had a white fur collar!

My very first paid job was when I was twelve years old. I worked Saturday nights from 7 P.M. to 11 P.M. at the dime store in Weslaco. My salary was fifteen cents an hour, but I only received fifty-nine cents in my little brown envelope because of one cent withheld for Social Security. Every Saturday I would buy a forty-nine-cent Nancy Drew mystery book, and still had ten cents left! That was enough for a five-cent movie and popcorn on a Saturday afternoon.

God Had Given Me a Brain and I'd Better Learn to Use It
Gayle Hunt

My dad was a farmer. He grew cotton in West Texas in the 1930s during the Depression. We later moved to East Texas where he worked in the oil fields, but he also farmed. Some of my earliest memories are of going to the fields to help my dad.

I have picked cotton, set out acres of tomato plants, and later picked green tomatoes to take to the packing shed. I have picked cucumbers and black-eyed peas by the bushel. We also had a huge garden where we grew all of our fruits and vegetables that had to be harvested and then canned or put up in fruit jars. Sometimes we got up really early before the sun came up so that we could be through before the sun got too hot. Sometimes we stopped work during the day, and then went back out late in the evening when it was cooler.

I was a child when I did this, starting at about nine or ten years old and working all through my teen years. I have buried all the feelings I felt about this as it was happening, and it is hard to recall just what I was feeling at the time. I do remember that I was the only one of us girls that had to go out in the fields and work like this. The other girls got to stay at the house.

I am not sure how this has impacted my life, although I know that it has. I do know that it was boring, difficult, and challenging. Rewarding? I guess it was rewarding in the sense that I did get to eat some of the fruits of my labors. I guess it can best be described as the most valuable work I have ever done because I knew that I didn't want to spend the rest of my life working in the fields. I didn't know how to make life better then, but I knew I had to find a way. I also knew that God had given me a brain, and if I wanted a better life, I had better learn to use it.

❈ Making My Own Way
Erma Hiltpold

Long before I finished high school, I was preparing myself and counting the days to find a job. Unlike most girls at that age, I wasn't thinking of marriage. That would have to wait. What was uppermost in my mind was to carry my own weight, to make my own way. The details of how it all came about are vague. I only remember the small office adjacent to a lumberyard and cotton gin. A desk and telephone with a comfortable chair were assigned to me. I welcomed the feeling of responsibility.

My employer and I had already agreed my starting salary would be six dollars a week with room and board. My hours would be 7 A.M. to 7 P.M.

On the day before my first day on the job my father drove me to my employer's home. There, I met his wife, who welcomed me, at the same time directing me to a small room with a back entrance to their modest bungalow.

"The room is small," she said, "but you'll have a lot of privacy. On his short visits from college, my nephew found it much to his liking."

I was thinking, "In all of my eighteen years I've never had a room of my very own." Then I said, "It is good of you to explain. I will be most comfortable here, I can assure you!"

I started unpacking my satchel and thought to ask, "Could you let me borrow an alarm clock until I have time to purchase one?" When she left to get it, I thought about the hour. I would get up at 6 A.M., dress, eat breakfast, and then walk to the office some fifteen or twenty blocks away.

When I arrived at work, my employer was already there. "You have much to learn," he began. "You must learn how to write receipts, handle money, make the proper change, quote the price of lumber per foot and learn the difference between a four-by-four plank and a two-by-four."

I listened closely and soon caught on to the simple arithmetic of measurements and costs. I gloried in the responsibility as well as my independence.

Clerking in My Dad's General Store
Pat Simmons

During World War II, I started my first paid job, clerking in my dad's general store. My granddad, uncle, and dad had a hardware, grocery, and sporting-equipment business in our small community called Coopersdale. The business had been there since the late 1800s and was a strong influence on my childhood.

Every Saturday morning after I started the seventh grade, I would report to the store to help with the customers. It was my duty to go fetch the groceries ordered by the customers who came in to the store, sent notes with their children, or called in an order to be delivered. I assembled bread, eggs, milk, canned goods, flour, and so on, and then tallied up the bill by adding it in my head. Since I was very good in math, I could add the bills without error. My dad taught me to correctly make change and collect ration coupons.

I was very proud to be so helpful on such a busy day as Saturday. Most people were working during the war, so in spite of the shortages of meat, sugar, and fresh food, most people had money to spend. Dad taught me how to greet the customers and a lot about business. I worked at the store on Saturday for five years and at the end of each Saturday, collected my wages of one dollar.

❋ "I'm Doing the Best I Can"
Patricia Gunderlach

I kept up the tradition of working woman/wife established by my grandmothers and their mothers, although I did not know it until long after I was an adult. One grandmother was a secretary in the State Legislature; the other was a career teacher and school principal because she had the advantage of two degrees. One great-grandmother was a nurse before she married; the other shared the onerous drudgery of farm life in South Dakota. In fact, one of her sons would make a name for himself writing novels and short stories about the hardships of rural life in that area.

A counselor once told me that if you want to understand yourself as a woman, take a close look at the previous three generations. I did, and discovered their pattern and how I fit into it.

Working for my dad in his office from 1953 to 1958 gave me lots of experience—staying focused, staying mentally limber and ready to take on any project put to me, staying the course, and learning to work with other employees as well as with the public. At first I was a file clerk, filing particular insurance rates in eighteen volumes in which few people ever looked. I was twelve years old when I came diagonally across the street from Sidney Lanier Junior High School at 3:35 P.M. each workday, no matter the weather. I earned fifty cents an hour and could treat myself to a Coke from the vending machine in the little kitchen used for employees' break time. Often when I sat at the small chrome kitchen table, someone would already be deeply into a story about her husband or her children or her parents. Like a toad in the punch, I sat quietly, drinking my Coke, until I had finished and could leave. At first, some of the story-tellers would change the subject when I popped in for a few minutes; but later everyone had concluded that I told no tales, so they talked about all kinds of subjects—even about my dad, who was their boss.

Later I made arrangements for my best friend, Marsha Harris, to work with me in that tiny, cramped office. We shared the work and the pay. Then, neither Marsha nor I could afford a Coke, so we went straight to the task. The room was so small that it could not accommodate a third person, and it was paneled in such dark wood that we had trouble seeing the minuscule print. Later I hoped that we had done an accurate job of it; if we pasted some of the rates in wrong places, it was an accident attributed to inadequate lighting.

The next year I was in training to become a relief switchboard operator. My dad's insurance business took up three-quarters of a small two-story building, so a switchboard was the most efficient way to handle all of the calls. The switchboard was the only fixture in the foyer except for a sofa where people sat, waiting for an envelope or for an employee to take them into the inner sanctum.

The board was about four feet tall and about three feet wide and eighteen inches deep, with maybe forty cords. The green ones were to answer an incoming call, and the red ones were to connect an employee's phone to the outside. A few times a year the board would be silent for three to five minutes or so. The rest of the time the operator had to hop, skip, and all but run in place to answer the insistent incoming calls, with their flashing lights and beeping tones, and simultaneously connect several employees to an outside line.

Then there were the employees who wanted to talk directly with the operator about a customer who was scheduled to come in shortly. Their lights flashed and their buzzers beeped, and the operator had to learn to identify the tiny differences in tones in order to answer them correctly.

As if that were not enough, the western one-quarter of the building was rented to lawyers who typified type A personalities, and each of them had a telephone on the operator's desk and expected A+ service. The operator had to rig the bells in each of those telephones not only so they had distinctly different sounds, but also so they rang more quietly so their noise would not squash the various sounds of the board. Meanwhile, customers were entering and leaving the building, asking questions and letting in noisy street din with the open door.

And finally, there was my daddy, the boss. He demanded A+ service from his operators and paid them well to keep them. If his flashing light was not answered almost immediately, he would be bellowing on the squawk box—a direct line from his desk to the operator's desk. "What's the matter down there? Why haven't you answered my line?" And I was in training at thirteen to learn to operate this communications system, the central nervous system of the business.

As relief operator, I worked the board only fifteen to twenty minutes every afternoon, while the regular operator took a break. But the scene can become chaotic in moments, and then those few minutes loom long into the future for an overwhelmed operator. Usually I did well enough, and my mistakes were accepted with good grace—unless one of those mistakes involved one of the lawyers with the "race horse" personality.

One day I had my trial by fire. The board was especially busy and at that instant my dad's light flashed and he asked for a conference call. All of a sudden, I could not remember the first of several steps necessary to grant his request. Lights flashed all over the board, tones beeped—some needed to be unhooked since their call was completed, some needed an outside line, some needed to be connected to another employee, and on and on. Incoming customers were stacked three deep waiting their turn to tell me what they needed. And I sat there, paralyzed, trying to remember how to sequence the steps to make a conference call. In a very few seconds, my daddy's booming voice seemed to loom out of the squawk box and demandingly hover over my frozen body. That woke me up! I flipped the switch and did not quite yell back, "I'm doing the best I can!"

Total silence followed. The lights quit flashing, the tones quit beeping, and the customers patiently waiting might have been sculpture. Had I dared to talk back to the boss? In that blessed silence I remembered how to rig a conference call, did it, and quietly informed Daddy on the squawk box that his call was ready, in my most professional, demure voice.

Neither of us mentioned the episode when Daddy drove us home after work.

District 23, Speedway School
Rose Urba

I came home from college in May 1931. The family was suffering from the Depression and I was told I could not go back to college. I must find a job.

I was qualified to teach all grades in country school. I had my certificate verifying this. In those days the county was divided into districts. Each district had its board of directors. They were authorized to tax property, and it was up to them to decide on the policy of the school. They hired the teacher, set the teacher's salary, and set up a budget to operate the school. The board that granted my job request was in District 23, Speedway School, ten miles south of David City, Nebraska, where I lived. They offered me seventy-five dollars a month. No one would "room-and-board" me in the area, as was the custom in many districts. That was okay because I could stay at home and drive the ten miles. With the help of my dad I bought a secondhand Chevy —no heater, no radio—and took driving lessons. I give credit to my guardian angel for watching over me as I traveled all those miles in all kinds of weather in a car poorly equipped.

The school was one of the best in the county. It was a wooden building, painted white, with windows all along the north side, a furnace in the basement, a telephone, electricity, a piano, a pump for fresh water outside the front door, and an outhouse fifty yards away, hidden in big trees.

I was in seventh heaven. I had twelve students—five girls and seven boys. One of my first grade boys came to school and did not speak English. He spoke Czech—a real challenge for me. His older sister helped us to communicate.

Pupils were dismissed for the day at 4 P.M. Most of them walked home. Then I set the room in order, emptied the water cooler, swept the floor, and made plans for teaching the next day before I started for home. The books were adequate, and my budget allowed paper, construction paper, glue, and sweeping compound. Workbooks were too expensive, so I made all of my exercises and work projects. I used a hectograph to make copies. A hectograph is a gelatin substance in a tray about ten by sixteen inches. Purple ink is used for the original copy, which is transferred to the gelatin surface. Copies can then be made.

The classes were small, which made for little competition. It was a challenge to keep the students motivated. All classes were held in the room in which the students were studying, so it was possible to learn a lot from each class just by listening. My students studied diligently and did well in the required state and county tests. They always had a good showing of projects and art at the county fairs. Besides the required curriculum, I taught the girls to crochet and embroider. The boys did woodworking —birdhouses, small boxes, picture frames.

I visited the parents and discovered many young people in the community. None of them were going to high school. I thought, what a tragedy and what a waste of talent. I called a meeting and suggested that we pool our talents and present a three-part comedy play to the community. The idea was accepted. We did this for two years. Winter months were now used to study and rehearse the parts. We had a wonderful time. It brought the community together and cemented many friendships. We practiced at the schoolhouse evenings and Sunday afternoons. A hall was rented for the presentation of the production in a small community town of Brainard, Nebraska. Tickets were printed, and we advertised. A large audience enjoyed the presentations, and stars were born. We all had a good laugh. It was great fun. Both projects brought a good feeling of community comradeship.

I was treated very well by the whole community. They shared their produce, like potatoes, onions, eggs, sweet corn, and apples. I was remembered very well at Christmastime. Easter and my birthday brought a cake baked and decorated by one of the mothers, Allie. These gifts were so special and delicious.

My success was partly due to the cooperation of the parents. They upheld my discipline decisions. I loved those children! Many of them had never been to a movie, nor attended any social functions other than family gatherings. With the help of my parents, I would entertain a couple at a time for a week and in my home. They enjoyed my younger siblings, a picnic, and a good movie. I took them on field trips to our State Capitol building in Lincoln and to the state penitentiary and to a newspaper. Their world was expanding.

One of the girls, Elsie, graduated from eighth grade. She passed all the county tests with honors. She wanted to be a teacher. Her parents had the notion that girls do not need an education (this was in the 1930s), so, at fourteen, she was destined to be a stay-at-home farm girl. I couldn't accept that. I visited with her parents and convinced them to let Elsie come back to school in the fall. She and her younger sister walked one and one-half miles. I taught her English and some music, and she helped with the other students. The next year her parents sent her to high school and she became a country-school teacher, her wish. Elsie married, and her husband was killed in the Korean War. She had a son, who was an engineer. He committed suicide. I don't know the circumstances. She continued to care for her parents, who moved from the farm to a nice home in David City. God bless Elsie!

Last week I received a letter from her. She wrote about her flowers, vegetable garden, and three of her Speedway classmates. She told me that Speedway District 23 is no more. The building is now a private home in David City. Her last paragraph warmed my heart. She writes, "It was so wonderful to have you for our teacher. You did so much for us. And that includes your mother and father. Thank you. I have the clothespin bag we made at school and use it yet. Things are not so easy for me, but I keep going and with prayer I make it from day to day and that is good."

Times were rough in those days. We were all in "deep depression" economically. My salary took a downward fall and it was now fifty dollars a month. Teachers were everywhere, and they all wanted jobs. I was underbid at forty-five dollars a month. My teaching days at Speedway were over. I was very sad to leave my students. They had done so well scholastically and had given me a feeling of accomplishment. I know I made a difference. The challenges were many and matured my thinking. I was sad to leave Speedway.

Southern Belle: A Full-Time Job
Marthanne Buzader

I was raised to be a hostess and a wife and mother. All other work felt inappropriate. You can't go against your raisings. I was brought up as a southern belle.

Plenty of people had more money than we did, and my mother knew exactly who they were. I got the impression that they were the good people. (My father called them rich bitches.) But we all had Negro maids and yardmen and garbage collectors. Mother also knew who was good help and who was not. Having help allowed us to continue a lifestyle of parties akin to antebellum days.

Mother made me a new dress for almost every party. She gave wonderful parties on my birthdays. She gave impromptu parties probably every week. She entertained her bridge club and supper club and church circle and Daddy's office staff and the relatives and my friends and my brothers' friends. She threw a July Fourth party every year that lasted from dawn into the night. She entertained for weddings and funerals and new babies and dove season and when someone caught a bunch of fish.

It was small wonder I grew up thinking that women were supposed to hostess. That's the work required to get to go to more parties. And it was work. You had to look good and make sure everyone had a good time. You cooked all the food and did all the cleanup and planned games and made decorations. It was a full-time job.

Generally, you learned to be a hostess before you learned to be a mother. At the time I did not know that either was work, because it was clear that mothers did not work. The women in town who had to work were to be pitied somehow, so you bought Avon products from them or went to them to get your hair done.

Mother sure did work. She worked hard almost all the time, and she was good at what she did. She excelled at cooking and sewing and child rearing. Everyone said so. She even learned to type and helped Daddy at the office during World War II, but that was an extension of her job as wife and helpmate.

Certainly I learned a lot about being a hostess and a wife and a mother. I also learned that other work, including housecleaning, was somehow lesser. My work outside the home, as we learned to say in the sixties, could therefore never be as meaningful as homemaking. Even when there was no more South, no more help, and eventually no more husband, I had a difficult time honoring my other work. It meant you had to work, that the family had fallen on hard times, or was under duress, such as Mother's job in World War II.

A Fitting Job
Mathilda Mimun

(Mathilda Mimun, a non-native speaker of English, asked that her writing appear unedited.)

When I came to Austin after my divorce my daughter's mother-in-law helped me very much from the very first day. Mrs. Kruger found me a job at Ivey Wade dress shop very exclusive shop. I did a lot of alterations before in San Antonio but never made fitting. They accepted me right away in my department. There was another lady her name was Merle and she was very nice to me.

The first time they ask me to take a fitting I was very nervous, but Merle encouraged me. She told me, "Go on, you can do it." So I did. This lady had a problem with her dress. I wasn't sure what I'm doing and I figure it out, but I was praying I was doing the right thing. Well, the alteration was a success and I was very proud of my self.

Merle was giving me lots of encouragement and teach me many thing. I worked with her for five years. Then she retired. So they have to look for someone else to replace her. They found an Italian woman, she was very good with her work and she was fast working but she was very hard getting along with her. She made my life miserable. She was like two personalities, one time she was very nice and sweet an other time she is mean, telling me thing to hurt my feeling. She was very jealous of me. Anything I do she want to do the same. Like if I take one day off for some reason she have to take off whether she need it or not.

A Cattle Drive
Erin Colleen Moore

Our ranch was twelve miles from town. When I was a kid, neither we nor our customers had trucks large enough to haul the cattle to market, as they do now. So they got there by walking —and someone had to drive them.

After the animals to be sold were collected and separated from the others into a small pasture, we got up very early in the morning, saddled the horses, and started out. I was, I guess, twelve to sixteen years old. Since it was usually fall, I would wear a blue jean jacket over my shirt, and blue jean pants, and boots and a cowboy hat. I did not saddle the horse, but I did everything else myself. We sometimes packed a lunch, or sometimes it would be brought in a pickup.

We collected the cattle and drove them through the gate of the small pasture into the big pasture. We followed them along the road, heading off any that tried to stray in the wrong direction. As the day progressed, it would get hot and we would get more tired. We passed two or three more fences, and finally, about four in the afternoon, we reached the railroad stock pens. There the cattle would be sorted into carloads—young steers in one, old cows in another, and so on. Finally, the switch engine would pull a cattle car up to the gate of the pen, where a ramp allowed the cattle to walk up into the car. Then we would go by the drugstore for some ice cream, and Mother would pick us up in the car to go home. I think a hired man would usually take the horses back the next day.

 # The Autoclave
Lavern Crawford

Surgical nursing was the most difficult work I have ever done, and it took up forty-three years of my life's work! Sterilization is the key word in maintaining a sterile field for an operation. This job was done by the O.R. nurse.

Several methods of sterilization were used: boiling water, boiling oil, chemicals, alcohol lamp, or steam under pressure. Steam under pressure was my challenge! Consider a barrel-sized pressure cooker, named an autoclave, lying on its belly. It had a double chamber: one chamber for supplies like linen packs, etc., and the second chamber for the steam. In the smaller hospitals there was no direct steam supply, so to obtain steam one had to light the boiler (located under the chamber) and get the water boiling enough to get enough pressure to sterilize all the instruments being used. This was a very tricky job, but I became very skilled at it—I guess it was my forte. It required that we keep one eye on the boiler and pressure gauge while we continued to do the rest of the tasks of getting ready for the operation.

Once, an attendant rushed through the room where I was working with the autoclave; it was in a room between two operating rooms. The attendant had an almost empty can of ether that had been used in one room, and tossed it into the trash can right beside the open flame under the boiler! The ether exploded and shot the can straight up to the ceiling! We were lucky there was only a trace of ether left or we could have had a real explosion!

For the first ten years of my nursing career, I had to deal with the autoclave. My children used to say they could tell by the way I walked in the door what had been going on at work: "Oh, Mom's had a time with the autoclave today!" they would exclaim. It sure made me appreciate the hospitals in larger cities and the newer methods where you had steam piped directly into the operating room!

My Navy Career
Joan H. Crews

In the year 1943 I was attending Mayfair Taylor Secretarial School in Austin, Texas. It was rather boring, and I suppose I was looking for adventure. One day I decided to go join the Lady Marines. Since the Marines were a part of the Navy, they had a joint recruiting office. To this day I haven't figured out what happened, but I ended up being sworn into the U.S. Navy. Now I was a WAVE.

In May 1943, I received my orders to report to boot camp in New York City. I, who had never been out of the state of Texas, boarded the train and set out to see the world. I had no idea what lay ahead of me in boot camp.

The Navy had commandeered Hunter College, located in the Bronx, and many of the multistoried apartment buildings surrounding the campus. I, along with seven other girls, was assigned to an apartment on the seventh floor of our building. There was no furniture, just bunks and a locker for each girl. We were not allowed to smoke in our apartment. The smoking room was on the fourth floor. However, there was very little time out for smoking. We were allowed to use the elevator to carry our luggage up the day we arrived. That was the last time I saw the elevator. From then on, we climbed those seven flights of stairs!

Every day was filled with orientation classes, swimming classes, learning to march—it went on forever. The streets of the campus were all one-way, so if you had a class next door you might have to fall in and march four blocks to get back around to the building next door. It was all planned to teach us discipline and how to march. I felt honored when I was picked to be the Right Guide for my platoon.

Here I must tell about our uniforms. We were issued navy blue cotton gabardine uniforms and cotton stockings. When we marched, those cotton skirts clung to the cotton stockings and walked right up our legs. About every ten steps, in unison we had to bend down and pull our skirts down. What a sight!

After a full day of activity, we usually went back to our barracks to freshen up for evening chow. Climbing those seven flights of stairs was not easy, but when you looked around and no one else was dropping out, you just kept going. One day I had five minutes to spare so I fell onto my bunk and thanked

God for that five minutes. It didn't last! The fire bell rang! We had to grab a blanket, run down all those stairs, up a hill to the next block, and muster for roll call. Following the drill we had to go back down the hill, up those seven flights of stairs to return the blankets, then back down the stairs, muster for roll call, and march to the mess hall for evening chow.

I did some pretty dumb things, such as rolling up my hair every night, even though I had a swim class first period every morning. Another thing I did: when I was going north on the train, a black person sat down beside me, so I got up and moved. Just ignorance. I grew up in a small town in Texas where there were no black people, and I had heard that whites did not associate with blacks. Another awakening occurred one day when I returned to the barracks and several of my friends were crying. I asked what was wrong and was told that six of our girls had been kicked out and already sent home because they were lesbians. Well, surprise, surprise. I didn't even know what they were talking about.

After four weeks of training we were given a pass to go into New York City. We always had to go everywhere in a group, never alone. We decided to eat at a place called Hamburger Heaven. We didn't have much money, and back in Texas you could buy a hamburger for twenty-five cents. Imagine the shock when my bill for one hamburger was four dollars and ninety-five cents.

One day when I was walking my guard post, a handsome young Annapolis cadet came by, so I snapped to attention and saluted him. He was so surprised that he stopped to chat. It was strictly against the rules for a guard to talk to anyone. I was lucky no one saw me. Anyway, it turned out that the young man was home on leave. He lived nearby and invited me to his home for dinner with his family. I don't remember how I managed to get a pass, but I did. It was a very interesting evening. His father and sister (there was no mother) had never been out of New York, and they seemed quite intrigued at meeting someone from Texas. They thought we all rode in covered wagons, wore boots, and carried guns.

Eventually boot camp came to an end and we were to go to various schools. I had asked to go to Link Trainer School, but unfortunately I scored higher in mechanical ability than teaching ability. I was sent to Aviation Metalsmith School in Norman, Oklahoma.

On a hot July day we boarded a coal-fired train in New York headed for Norman. This was before air conditioning, so all the windows were open, the seats were straight-back hardwood with no cushions, and no recliners. We slept sitting straight up and soon learned to lean over and brush away the cinders before opening our eyes.

Because we were women and considered nonessential to the war effort, every time we met a troop train heading east, we had to pull off the track to a siding and wait for it to pass. Because there were lots of troop trains, we spent many hot hours just sitting on a sidetrack. Believe it or not, it took us five days to go from New York to Oklahoma City. During that time I have absolutely no recollection of eating. I have no idea whether we had a dining car or ate box lunches.

Eventually, we arrived in Oklahoma City at about 2 A.M. No one was there to meet us to take us to the Naval Air Station near Norman. There was an inviting little park across the street from the train station, and since we were all exhausted, we went over and collapsed on the grass while we awaited our transportation. By the next day, we all became aware that the pretty little park was infested with chiggers, and now we were too.

We arrived at Norman about 3 A.M. and were assigned to our barracks. Upon entering, someone turned on a light. Immediately we heard a loud command, "Blow out that light," so we all went to bed in the dark.

At 5 A.M. someone entered the barracks and routed us out to go to the mess hall for KP duty. Normally, each group of new students was assigned to KP duty for two weeks. Then they started to school and another group came to relieve them. Unfortunately for us, they decided to close the school in Memphis and transfer those WAVES to Norman. The rule was that once you started to school you could not go on KP. Well, all the girls coming from Memphis had started to school; therefore, our group was stuck on KP for three months.

Shortly before our three months were up I got a sore throat and was sent to the hospital for a tonsillectomy. Not one to loaf around, I started helping on the ward. Whenever the doctors came each morning for their rounds, I was always making beds, mopping, or some such chore, so they didn't know I was a patient. Twenty-one days went by before I finally asked when I could leave. Of course I was released immediately.

When I reported to school, I was told they were closing Metalsmith School to WAVES and the last group was already nine weeks into the course. Since I'd had some experience working at the Naval Air Station in Corpus Christi, I told them I already knew what they had covered. They gave me tests, which I passed with flying colors, so I joined the class of six girls and ninety-one men. I graduated with honors and made the highest grade in the course ever made by a WAVE. I completed the twenty-one-week course in eleven weeks.

I was then assigned to the assembly and repair department at the Naval Air Station on North Island, San Diego, California. I was put in a shop where I was the only girl working with fifty-four men. Our mission was to repair the fighter planes brought in on the carriers from battles in the Pacific. If replacement parts were not available from the supply room, we checked out the parts and made replacements. If parts were unavailable, we checked out the blueprints and made the part. Our accuracy tolerance had to be within a few thousandths of an inch. Every job was different and challenging, but very essential to the war effort.

There were many funny incidents that happened during my hitch in the Navy; however, one in particular stands out. One day at the mess hall in San Diego, we were served some delicious-looking butter beans. I didn't know they were boiling hot, and when I put a spoonful in my mouth, one huge bean stuck to the roof of my mouth. Of course, it burned a big blister just the size of the bean. The blister soon burst and my mouth was so sore I could not eat. I decided I needed to go to the dispensary for medication. I didn't want to tell them I didn't have sense enough to spit out hot beans, so I just said I had a sore in my mouth. The doctor looked in my mouth and was horrified. He said it was the biggest canker sore he had every seen and was caused by lack of vitamin B. He then called in a class of medical corps trainees to view my mouth and gave them a long lecture on canker sores. By then I was too embarrassed to confess the real problem. The doctor then painted my "canker sore" with tincture of violet and gave me a prescription for some B vitamins. The tincture of violet promptly healed my "canker sore" and I never filled the prescription for the B vitamins. (I wonder why you never hear of tincture of violet anymore—it really works.)

During my two years in San Diego I formed some close and long-lasting relationships. I look back on those years with fond memories and wish that I could reunite with some of my teammates.

On August 6, 1945, an atomic bomb was dropped on Hiroshima. The word spread quickly throughout our shop. I could not comprehend anything of that magnitude, therefore I did not believe it. I was sure it was propaganda. Not until three days later, August 9, 1945, when the second bomb was dropped on Nagasaki, did I realize that the war was essentially over. It was the end of an era and the beginning of a new life for me.

When the war ended in 1945, my fiancé returned from Europe and we were married on October 15, 1945. I then applied for my discharge. The Navy policy was that if you were married and your husband had just come back from overseas, you were granted an immediate discharge. I fit those criteria. My husband was career Army, so I spent the next twenty-eight years moving from place to place with the Army.

An Office in the Courthouse
Margaret C. Long

For many years my husband was in the habit of coming to the house, dirty and tired, and would watch our little children while I was sent to the county seat, about twenty miles away, usually to buy parts for whatever he was fixing. Sometimes he would fill in a form and sign it, requesting a short-term demand loan from the bank because he was going the next day to buy cattle or heavy equipment. He would tell me exactly what he wanted to do and I knew the answers to any questions the banker might ask. Invariably, the banker would hem and haw and then say that my husband would have to come in himself and tell him about it before he could approve the loan.

This frustration went on for several years. Then I began working for the Department of Public Welfare, and I had an office in the courthouse. The banker was also an attorney, and he had occasional business in the courthouse. One day when he walked by, he saw me and stopped to say hello. He was obviously surprised to see me there, and I felt that he was impressed with my corner office with large windows and a secretary in the outer office. I found out just *how* impressed when he approved the loan the very next time I was sent to request one.

 Things Began to Change
Faye B. Kelly

In the fall of 1962, I got a teaching position in the Department of Literature at American University. Little did I know or even suspect that this position would not only be a rewarding teaching experience but would propel me into the fight for women's rights. Until this time, if I had been discriminated against, I was unaware of it.

Early in my second year the chairman of the department had to have a serious operation, followed by a long convalescence.

He asked me to be acting chairman, but not to tell anybody—an absolutely untenable position, but I tried.

One of the first things I did was to seek out the budget for the department. Lo and behold, all the men (even the single ones) in the department were paid more than the women, even if the women had higher qualifications and more experience. I copied the budget and gave a copy to every woman in the department. We organized as a group but remained so for only a little while because women faculty from other departments heard about us and asked to join. Soon all female faculty members were in the group.

One of our first tasks was to elect women to the faculty senate. At the time, there were only three or four women full professors in the entire university—about four hundred faculty. After we had enough women members in the senate to have a voice, we changed the makeup of the Faculty Relations Committee, which passed on all promotions and tenure. At that time, only full professors could be members of this committee. We voted to have associate professors as members of this committee.

I was soon made a member. The men all looked at me as if they expected me to come in with elbows askew and eyes blazing. Instead, I served the coffee and sandwiches (furnished by the university). The next year, I was voted chairman of the committee. Even I was amazed at the tactics some of the department chairmen would use, rather than promote a woman. They would refuse to recommend or send the papers to the Faculty Relations Committee. But now that all women faculty had been sensitized, some woman would alert the committee about eligible women, and the committee chairman would send for folders of the eligible women. They would review the qualifications and ask in writing, with a copy to the Dean, as to why the woman was not recommended. Things began to change.

My Silver Star
Billie Grace Herring

Having grown up in a time when the favorite reward in school was a star on a chart for whatever the teacher was trying to encourage you to learn, I guess I decided that stars were "good." Of course, having to do everything perfectly so my parents would be proud of me also contributed to the "star mentality."

In 1986, I was an associate professor and Associate Dean of the Graduate School of Library and Information Science at UT. I had despaired of ever attaining the rank of full professor because my research record was much less than stellar. I had preferred to focus on teaching well, on public service, and on advising and counseling students. When my Dean, Ron Wyllys, insisted that I prepare a dossier of my accomplishments and allow myself to be nominated for promotion, I was terrified. Preparing that promotion dossier was the hardest thing I had done in my career. Most of the preparation was done in the wee hours of the morning when I couldn't put it off any longer. It was scary and painful to review my career in such scrutinizing detail. The task was especially exacerbated by the fact that I was just beginning to recover from a deep major depression. I had no confidence in myself and felt hopeless.

To encourage me, my husband bought me a faceted Waterford paperweight for my desk at home. His card said, "I believe in you. Believe in yourself."

The dossier was finished, the promotion went forward, and I became a full professor. I remember the day that the decision was made at a conference between Ron, the university president, the provost, and the vice president for graduate studies. I was beside myself with anxiety and described my feelings as something like the sounds of the chickens in Mussorgsky's "Pictures at an Exhibition." When Ron left a bottle of champagne on my desk, I assumed that I had been promoted. I figured that if I had not been promoted, he would have left me a six-pack of beer to drown my sorrows.

The year before, I had seen a silver star pin by Paloma Picasso in the Tiffany catalog that I really liked. I decided to celebrate my promotion by buying myself the stylized sterling silver star pin. I had never spent three hundred dollars on anything for myself. But I have loved the pin, wear it regularly, and am pleased that I finally treated myself.

 ## Just an Old Hooker
Lois Earley

We were living in West Lafayette, Indiana, and had a one-year-old daughter and a three-year-old son. I was in my late twenties and getting twitchy, because I had nothing of substance to occupy my mind and imagination. There was always the laundry to do and housework to keep up, but when you have read one cleanser can, you've read them all. There is no mystery left. We had little money to spare, and my husband drove our only car to the university where he taught every day. I was stranded at home with two toddlers unless I was willing to take them on the bus. That was so hard that I did not do it very often.

One day after walking back from the market, I sat with my lunch and trolled through *Family Circle* magazine, which I had just bought (I think it cost all of thirty-five cents in those days). There on the page before my eyes was a picture of a rug that was perfect for our living room. It couldn't cost much, could it? It was absolutely what that sparsely furnished room needed, but I hadn't known it until I saw it. Had you put a gun to my head I could not have described what was required, and here it was —and in living color! What color! What design! I must have it. I could hardly stand it until my spouse returned from his office.

When my husband (otherwise known as His Honor) came home, I showed the picture to him with great excitement. I just knew he would say that it would be tight, but that we would manage to get it somehow. Wrong. He said that if I wanted it,

I would have to make it. I was bitterly disappointed, then angry, then determined—determined, but ignorant of the process of rug making. There were no rug clubs around, but eventually I found an advertisement for a book on rug hooking and I ordered it: *How to Hook Rugs*, by Pearl McGown. That book tasted like one more, so I ordered the second one, *Color in Hooked Rugs*, by the same author, and dove headlong into the complexities of color and balance. In the meantime, I had begun to scour Red Cross outlets and Goodwill Stores for used woolen clothing to use in making the rug. When the second-hand stores found out why I was buying the old coats, skirts, and jackets, they refused to sell to me any longer. By that time I was in a braider's club, and it was great. They had to have long, thin strips so I inherited their short leftovers.

My husband built a frame four and one-half feet wide on which I could roll the burlap and I was on my way to making a four-by-six-foot area rug. It's an old joke with me now, but when someone asks what I do that I really enjoy, I say that I am just an old hooker, you should pardon the expression. The room gets quiet instantly. Then, of course, I explain the word. This work became the most exciting thing in my life. I was playing with color and balance and texture. I would lie awake nights pondering the problems posed by the juxtaposition of colors and patterns. I felt alive for the first time in a very long time.

The fact that others did not share my enthusiasm nor see the value in what I did had no impact on me. This was for me, and I found it eminently satisfying. It kept me company during long days and nights watching the kids while my husband worked. It took the place of human communication in an unsociable neighborhood. It served as a good place to work out anger when things were stormy between His Honor and me.

I dyed some fabrics and stripped color from other fabrics. I toyed with stripes and plaids, but above all, I learned to take the garments apart in the garage or in the back yard. It was a very messy business.

At last I was about six months from the rug's completion. It had taken me almost two years to reach that point and I knew it was a success. But I still had not found what I needed for the border. The pattern was of assorted squares and rectangles, all hooked in earth colors. I needed a mottled border. One day in town I met a friend I had not seen in a couple of years. I said "Hi, Marilyn—may I have your coat?" She said yes.

It was perfect. Her coat was creamy off-white and light cinnamon small checks. Yummy. The rug had taken a little over two years to make, and had given me great pleasure and tension release. It's been on the floor for thirty years.

Granny's Biscuits
Sue Kinney

Laura Jennings Butler made the best biscuits and hotcakes in the world, and she was my "Granny." I once ate ten of her pancakes at one sitting—and they were not small pancakes.

Now I love to cook. It is one of my favorite things to do, and I have passed this love on to my children—the boys as well as the girls. They are all passionate cooks. I would love more than anything to give them the recipes for Granny's melt-in-your-mouth pancakes and her take-two-and-butter-them-while-they're-hot biscuits, but this cannot be. Oh, I could easily give them a list of the ingredients and their proportions, but the problem is, I couldn't tell them when or what to hum at just the right time. You see, part of Granny's secret to making these mouthwatering delights was humming a good old Methodist hymn while she worked.

Was it two cups of flour and la de da, da, la de da ("Rock of Ages") or da da, da, de, da da de da da ("I Walk through the Garden Alone")? And what went with the two heaping teaspoons of baking powder? Was it da da, da da, da, da ("Holy, Holy, Holy"), she hummed? Who knows? Those hymns were pieces of her heart that only she could add, and she did it by the loving cupful.

CHAPTER FOUR

Family

Grandmother and the Pirates

No matter how she defines family, no woman can evade its deep and enduring influence in her life. Her role within the family largely shapes her perception of self, and the family's characteristic patterns of interaction will structure her assumptions and expectations about human relationships.

Memories of family life reflect women's diverse experience in loving and secure families that shared joy and endured adversity together, and in troubled families and those assailed by tragedy. Women may regard family as a reliable safe haven, offering support and comfort from the tribulations of a cruel and unforgiving world, or something closer to a playing field, battleground, or prison. Interpersonal bonds among family members vary in intensity and duration, as familial relationships endure, break apart, become exclusive, become inclusive.

When we tell stories about our family, we pass along the family's explanations about who "we" are, how we came to live in a certain place, and why we occupy a certain social position. These valuable stories of courage and chicanery, animosities and forgiveness, endurance through long hardships, and times of tears and of triumph orient us within our family's complex network of relationships, teach of us our family's past, and help us understand our family's values. Not all the details may be literally true—in fact, much of the time, they are not. But they are believed, and that is what is important.

✿ Grandmother and the Pirates
Eula Rae McCown

My dad's mother, Jennie Menard Larrabee, died in 1955 at the age of ninety-six. She was born in 1859 on Clear Lake at Seabrook, Texas, in her grandfather's house. They were among the first settlers in Seabrook.

My grandmother was home alone at the age of sixteen, and all the rest of the family, with several servants, were working in the fields surrounding the house, when she heard voices carrying across the lake. When she went to the front window, she saw quite a large boat with approximately eight pirates rowing toward her home.

She was a fast thinker and did not have time to run for help, so she went into the kitchen. It had a large cast-iron wood stove with the utensils hanging from ceiling racks. She grabbed several heavy ladles and began beating on the stove and began yelling every man's name she could think of—"George! Jim! Bill! Get your guns!"—continually adding more boys' names. When she dared stop and go look out the window again, the pirates had turned their boat around and they were headed out of the lake.

We always thought if she had not seen them and taken the actions she did, the pirates would have raped her and stolen her away.

She was a very beautiful and gracious person, even as an old lady.

✿ My Father and the Value of Money
Bonnie Knipp

My father's family came over from France after the Civil War. His father Edward met and lived with an Indian girl named Stella. (Her father was a Cherokee chief.) They had a daughter named Sylvia. Edward's father made him marry Stella but, to remove the shame of this mixed marriage, bought them a plantation in Cuba, where my father, Henry, was born in 1891.

Edward died in a couple of years, and Stella moved back to the States. She could neither read nor write, so there is some question as to the spelling of our family name. My great-grand-father then bought Stella and her children a farm outside of San Francisco. He would come to see them and give Daddy money. One day, Daddy refused to accept the money, and this angered Stella. She told him, "I'll teach you the value of money," and gave Daddy to another farmer. He was just seven years old. He stayed there until he was about nine years old and then ran away.

Nanoo
Carole Burke

My grandmother, whom I called Nanoo, had a powerful influence on my life. One reason for this is that I contracted polio before I began to walk. My mother had younger children, so my grandmother took me to San Antonio for my weekly therapy, brace fittings, and all that went with it.

In looking back, I see that Nanoo tried to make these trips more fun for me by taking me to the places she loved and sharing them with me. We would go to antique shops: she knew them all. She took me to the Menger Hotel and told me all the history connected with it. She showed me the bar where Teddy Roosevelt recruited Rough Riders, and the picture over the bar that was loaned to the set of the movie *Giant*.

I always wanted to visit the baby alligators that lived in permanent residence there. A special treat was to eat lunch at the Camellia Room at the old Joske's near the Alamo. They served tiny sandwiches and had style shows at what was called luncheon time, and the ladies all wore hats and my grandmother always wore gloves.

When I was in the sixth grade, Nanoo took me to Warm

Springs in Georgia, and we rode the train. She had bought me a pillowcase so that I could learn to embroider. She told me it was very important for ladies to know how to do handwork. I think my grandmother knew from her own experience that for us to have lovely things in our homes, we had to be able to make them. And my grandmother loved pretty things.

So, as we rolled along with the beauty of the South going by, my grandmother taught me how to make French knots and satin stitch and chain stitch, and I learned that I loved it, too.

I don't think I ever finished that pillowcase. But over the years I have enjoyed and treasured pillows and pieces of needlepoint and embroidery I have created, along with the things that she gathered and saved for me, and that I live with now, every day.

 ## Grandma Maggie Helman
Joann Bynum

My grandmother lived in a tiny house next to us in Union City, Indiana. She dried corn and apples in bags and hung them in her woodshed. She made the best apple pies and sugar cookies.

Grandmother always had a quilt set up in her living room in front of the window. She quilted every day until she died. She made all the many grandchildren a quilt and quilted for other people and made a little extra money on the side.

In the winter I would stay overnight with her and sleep in the big brass bed with a down-filled mattress. She heated two bricks on the top of the living room stove, wrapped the bricks, and put them in the bed to warm our feet. In her kitchen she had an iron coal stove she cooked on and heated water from the well. She would start a fire every morning in the stove with a little kindling wood.

She made me a pink and white quilt with an embroidered bird in each square. The patterns came from a Sunday school paper we brought to her from church.

After a while Grandmother did not want to leave her house. She would sit at her table with a little radio on and listen to her favorite church sermon. She belonged to the Dunkard Church, now called the Church of the Brethren. She wore a net prayer-covering on her head. She wore five petticoats under her skirt and wore her hair in a tight bun on her head.

I remember one night when I had the croup and was gasping for my breath. I lay on the living room couch. My parents called the doctor and Grandmother was there. They thought I was going to die. Mother had lost her five-year-old brother from croup. Grandmother gave me some liquid on a spoon to make me throw up, then she gave me a spoon of sugar with a few drops of kerosene on it. She greased my chest with goose grease and kerosene. I got better and could breathe normally. The doctor did nothing but check me out and said I would be all right.

❁ My Mother and the Pigeons
Martha Knies

Mealtime at our house was always "Mother-inspired" because Mother was always there. Not Daddy, although we always set a place for him and hoped he'd make it before we all scattered.

Tonight was chicken and dumplings night. Mother did know how to stretch food. When the home extension agent came to teach Mother how to stretch her food dollars, she left early. She said Mother could teach her a few things, so down the road she went.

The chicken and dumplings were delicious—long, juicy, tender fingers of rolled-out dough, not punched pieces of canned biscuits or flour tortillas—and the meat had flavored the gravy broth just the way it should.

During the meal, George, or GW as we called him then, asked Mother if she knew what had happened to his pigeons. He said he'd been out to feed them and they weren't there. Mother said she didn't know what had happened. Perhaps a snake had crawled up and eaten them.

We kept eating. Soon the meal was finished. Daddy had not come home. The leftovers—really the best serving—were put aside for him. Mother always saw to it that his food was there.

Was this just another typical family supper? Well, it had been, until the next day, when GW discovered the feathers of his pet pigeons, the bones, scraps, and heads of every one of them. Dogs had uncovered this pigeon graveyard and revealed the secret source of our chicken and dumplings.

Today, when the survivors gather around the table, you can be sure we retell this story many times. Only today we can laugh about it, because today we understand Mother's love and sacrifices, and the terrible dilemma she faced. Feed the children or feed the pigeons her oldest son loved.

❧ An Unexpected Meeting
Patricia Lyón

Our firstborn was six months old. My mother (who thought that living in Bolivia meant that we were living in a thatched-roof hut) couldn't stand it any longer, got her passport, dug into the savings account, and got on a plane and came to see her first grandson. She felt she had to bring an appropriate gift, so she bought a stuffed life-sized chimpanzee. (I never knew why she picked that!) Mother always felt, when you were traveling, you had to be dressed properly: hat, gloves, and so on. She happened to have a mink cape, so that was part of her attire for the trip.

Mother was not due to arrive in Ciudad Bolívar (located on the edge of the Orinoco River) until that night, so José and I went into the city early to do some shopping and to visit his cousin. The Grand Hotel Bolívar was the only hotel in town and was the meeting place for all expatriates, no matter their nationality. José and I went there to get something to drink and also to make use of the bathroom.

I went into the seemingly empty bathroom and my nostrils were assailed by the scent of Lentheric's Tweed cologne—the only perfume my mother had ever used. I hesitantly said, "Mother?" (I never called her that—it was always Mum.) This mink-caped lady burst out of the stall, holding by the hand the stuffed life-sized toy chimpanzee, crying, "Pat!" And we fell into a loving embrace.

I miss her dreadfully!

William and the Outhouse
Martha Brian

I loved my cousin William. He was probably eighteen or nineteen years old when I was a tiny, lonely girl of six or seven, living in an isolated area of western Kansas that my father dubbed Rattlesnake Gulch.

We lived twenty-five miles from the nearest town and had no running water or electricity in our home. William came in the summers to help my father run the farm, work in the harvest, and take care of the cattle. He lived far away in Florida during the rest of the year. He was talented and kind and handsome. But best of all, he liked me! He talked to me, and with me, about all sorts of things no one else was interested in. He played his saxophone for me and he treated me with courtesy and a gentle humor. The other males in my life were rough-acting, harsh-speaking, impatient, and disinterested in me, except to tease or make fun of me. I was a tense, fearful, and easily startled child. My father nicknamed me "Spooky."

One afternoon my heart was so full of gratitude for William's kindness to me and for teaching me things that I decided to show him how much I appreciated him. I sat on top of the underground cyclone cellar and serenaded him with every song in my limited repertoire. I sang "Swing Low, Sweet Chariot," "Way Down upon the Swanee River," "Oh! Susanna," and "Little Brown Jug." I sang and sang my heart out to honor this very special man. Now, years later, I still flush with embarrassed awareness as I remember the self-conscious smile William gave me as he walked past me on the path from the outhouse where he had been trapped by my uninvited concert.

❀ My Brother Ray
Kathryn Doggett

Of my four older brothers, Ray is the one closest in age, as he is only two years older than I am. I remember he was always hitting me for entertainment—to hear me cry and tattle to Mother. I loved it when he got reprimanded and punished. When I was about eleven, I looked down at my chest on the left side and noticed it was rather bruised and swollen. I thought that Ray must have hit me there, so I tattled on him and he got a whipping from Mother.

A few days later I noticed the right side looked the same, so I tattled again. This time Mother figured it out and explained what was happening—I was in the first stages of becoming a young lady. She proceeded to help me make a little bra from a white flour sack.

I remember when Ray was a senior and I was a junior in high school. I was elected Football Sweetheart, and since he was the captain of the football team, the two of us rode around the football field before the game in a big convertible, smiling and waving to everyone. He would say (through smiling teeth), something like, "Get that stupid smile off your face—you look like an idiot." I didn't think so then, but I think now that he was secretly proud of me.

Today, Ray is in an Alzheimer's facility and has been for several years. I would love to hear him speak just a few words to me, regardless of what they were.

Aminta
Amparo González

When she was fifteen, my sister Aminta became much more than a sister to me. During my mother's long illness, our grand-mother was there for us, but soon after my mother died, we moved away. We went to live with an aunt while my father worked on the house which would be our own. It took a few months for the remodeling to be completed because materials were difficult to find during World War II. It was a house that my mother had inherited from her parents and probably dated back to the early 1900s, so it needed extensive work. My family was anxious to move into our house because my aunt had a family of her own and we felt we had worn out our welcome.

When the house was finally completed, Aminta was very happy to have a home and assumed the job of homemaker with pride and dignity. My father was able to continue farming and also opened a country store, which added to my sister's busy schedule. Although she had learned the basics of housekeeping at our aunt's house, the job she took on was one that would have scared the faint-hearted. From cooking to laundry, she did it all. My other sister, Alma, also quit school when she turned four-teen, to help my father at the store. I was to remain at the one-room country school, next door to our house, until it closed in 1949.

From the beginning, Aminta became my teacher and protec-tor. She taught me the necessity of keeping the house neat and clean, the importance of good grooming and wearing clothes which were not rumpled or sloppy. As well as sharing her bed with me so I wouldn't be afraid, she nursed me back to health when I was sick and held me when I cried.

She loved music, so the three of us would often sing songs on the hit parade or popular Mexican songs. The best time to sing was while washing dishes after supper. There were times when my father, who thought his girls were wonderful singers, would embarrass us by asking us to sing for his friends. What we really loved was to sing when we were piled up in the pickup truck, going somewhere. The three of us and my father would sing with gusto, never giving it a thought that every farm we passed could hear our harmony. You must remember, vehicles were not air-conditioned at that time.

When I went to school in town, the thirteen-mile ride on the bus required a very early start. Aminta made sure I was ready, had lunch money, and the courage to face the day. One thing she couldn't bring herself to tell me was about the facts of life. I was so embarrassed to tell her when I started my period. I kept discarding my soiled underwear. An outspoken girlfriend I had confided in came to the rescue. My sister was as serious as I when she told me what I must do thereafter.

During my first year of high school, Aminta got married and I was inconsolable. I cried when she and her new husband left on their honeymoon. Everyone thought it was so silly of me to grieve her leaving, but no one knew how lost I felt without her. I later realized she would be just a few miles away, so we could still see her often. I enjoyed her firstborn very much and took countless pictures of him. After I graduated, I even went to live with her and her husband for a while. It was during that time that I met my future husband, got married, and went to live in another state. Aminta was so happy when our first child was born, it wasn't surprising that they came to be with us. That was not an easy drive, since she had two children of her own and the trip took twelve hours.

As our families grew, we had many opportunities to spend time together. By this time, she had five boys and I had three boys and a girl. We camped and vacationed together on several occasions. Our children could not be loved more if she had been their grandmother. Her home was always the first place we would visit when we were in the area. Aminta started having heart problems during the 1960s. No one imagined the problem was serious, because she was still in her forties. I'm sure she had had problems for years, but it went undiagnosed until her first heart attack.

After more than twenty years in the military, we came home

to Texas and built a home in San Antonio. Aminta was so happy for us. I remember listening to the pride in her voice as she showed the house to another relative. She particularly enjoyed the bright, sunny kitchen. The trips became more infrequent, but despite her heart problems, she and the boys came to see our eldest son off when he left for a job in the Midwest. Her eyes were as full of tears as mine when the airplane lifted off.

Several surgeries and many years later her heart just gave out. As well as liking to sing, she also loved ballroom dancing and had always said she wanted to die at a party. Her wish came true one evening in 1981. She and her friend were visiting before the dancing started and she told her friend she was feeling a bit tired. Minutes later, she was gone. We drove to her home with our hearts breaking. I had lost a beloved sister and mother but, more than that, I had lost a friend.

We All Loved Each Other
Bertie W. Wright

My brother joined the Army and went off to World War I at age sixteen. My father tried to get him out because he was two years underage, but was unable to do so. At eighteen, he was back home, with his right limb off above the knee and lung damage due to having been gassed. I recall that my father, so concerned for my brother, would often get up in the night, go to the front yard fence, and openly weep.

Our transportation was walking and via buggy wagon and · horseback. Our movies were silent and Tom Mix, Mary Pickford, and Doug Fairbanks were our heroes. Sugar and flour were rationed, and also shoes. We lived mostly on food raised on the farm: poultry, beef, milk, and vegetables from the garden—when it rained. We used coal to heat and cook during the winter, and an oil stove in summer. We made lye soap for laundry and everything else. During this time we had a stepmother whom we all loved and who made a good home for us.

We were renting the farm. My dad worked so hard, but West Texas was not a kind area to farm. We were poor folks, but we were never cold or hungry or kept out of school to work. We all loved each other.

✿ Lillian
Francys Shliff

I was a teenager when Lillian arrived in California with her mother and brother. Her mother was my father's sister. She had lived in New York, was widowed, and cared for her mother for many years.

When they arrived in Los Angeles, I now became a part of my father's family. Lillian, my grown-up cousin, was a young woman and needed to find a job. She got a very interesting job, thanks to my father, in a specialty shop in Los Angeles. This would have been in the 1920s. Lillian wore beautiful clothes, which she was given by her employer. Lillian eventually handed them down to me.

I particularly remember the period when I was preparing for Confirmation and I had this gorgeous black coat with monkey-fur trim completely around the opening, and a white silk lining with black fabric enhancements. I was so dressed up and in so-phisticated adornment at fifteen, going to classes and preparations for my big day. Lillian brought many baubles and hand-me-downs to those impressionable years.

Then she married. Her husband was her college professor. Lillian had gone to law school at night after work, in spite of the complaints of two of her Los Angeles aunts. They thought she should be saving her money to support her mother and brother.

Lillian became a successful attorney, one of the first women attorneys in Los Angeles.

Rosy
Ruby Varnon Bishop

Rosy wore a sari and had thick, shining, black hair that hung to the back of her knees. She wore it up in a large bun at the back of her neck, and it was only after years of working for me that I saw her wear her hair down. Then she would tie a knot with her hair to keep it out of her face. She had beautiful black sparkling eyes that really set off a lovely smile that always seemed to be playing around her face. She was always singing as she worked and was always of such good cheer. She laughed so easily and was very quick with a reply. I remember one morning, my husband was complaining about combing his hair, and since it was beginning to thin, she said, "Big job, huh," and I almost fell off of the chair laughing. We were like kindred spirits, as our birthdays were only one day apart, separated by many years. This is her story.

Rosy was born in Bangalore, India, on September 5, 1922. She came from a well-educated family. Her father was a schoolteacher, and all her brothers and sisters went to university and were professional people. Rosy was the only one that did not get to finish her schooling. When Rosy was about ten years old, she had encephalitis. She was very ill for over six months, and her family did not know if she would live. She recovered, but she could not remember her studies. It was as if she had not gone to school and was going to have to start over. The nuns advised her family to take her out of school and train her for some task. Rosy had been with me for two years before she recounted this story. She still cried about not being able to go to school. Although she was in her thirties when I met her and could speak five languages, she still was unable to read or write any language.

She would often say to me, "Oh, Madam,"—that's what she called me—"I wish I could read the Bible." So one year that was my gift to her: teaching her how to read English, starting with the Bible. It was her dream to learn to read the Bible and to write a letter to her good friend Father Mathus. Until this time,

I always wrote her words, and when he replied, I would read his letters to her. I remember after reading his letter, I would give it to Rosy. She would kiss the letter and go to her room and place it in a special box where she put all her keepsakes.

Because Rosy did not have a formal education, her prospects for marriage were very poor, and when her family found a widower with a son, they thought it would be a good match. In fact, it was a very bad marriage. Her husband worked in the offices of the Indian Railway. This was a very good position, but he drank very heavily and money was scarce. When he became ill with liver disease, there was no money. India had no such thing as Social Security, and Rosy was sent out of the family home by her husband's sister. The only thing that she knew how to do was take care of a child. So she went to the YWCA in Bombay, where she got her first nanny position. Her first job was for an English family with a very sickly little boy. She worked for them thirteen years. Then they left and went to Hong Kong.

She heard that an American family needed a nanny, and she came to my door. The minute I saw how clean and well-spoken she was, I hired her. She had my children from the time they were small, and they were like her own. She played such a big part in their growing up. She often told me how much she loved my children, especially my daughter Danielle. When Danielle was only four years old, she made six yards of lace to be put around the bottom of her wedding slip. The lace was light blue, and it did go on the bottom of her wedding slip. She never spanked the children, and if they were acting up, she would only come to the door and click her tongue. They would look at her, and she would wag her finger and shake her head. They knew if she heard me correct them again, that she would march into the room and take their arm and lead them to the bedroom, where they would stay till bedtime.

After the children became too old for a nanny, she still stayed with us and ran the house. She awoke me every morning with a touch on my shoulder. "It's time to get up, Madam." There was always a breakfast tray on my reading table with a cup of tea and a slice of toast with jelly.

I taught Rosy how to cook. She would ask me each morning as I was leaving for work what I would like for dinner, and when I returned home, it would be ready. Rosy was so much a part of my family that she traveled with us on all our vacations, and our visits to the States. My family in the States knew her and wrote to her. They sent her birthday greetings, and mourned with us when she passed away on December 3, 1992. My children and I had a very sad Christmas that year. We had lost a beloved member of our family.

Even though Rosy never considered herself an educated person, when she died she could speak five languages and could read and write two. She had traveled around the world and had lived in Europe and the Middle East. She had been to Greece, and picked wild poppies around the base of the Acropolis. She'd been to Egypt, where they lost her luggage and all her saris, but she still enjoyed the ride on a camel to the base of the great Pyramids, and swam in the Mediterranean Sea. How blessed I was to have shared the joy of her life.

CHAPTER FIVE

Love
'Til We Meet Again

We don't know how or why various biological and cultural forces coalesce to make the stable, intimate connection so important to women. Love relationships matter so much that, for some women, they largely define self-identity. For others, shared intimacy may play an important, but not the sole or even central, role in their lives. Whatever its place, women typically care about intimacy, investing a great deal of effort in finding and keeping it.

Women born after the middle of the twentieth century have both enjoyed and struggled with the freedom to invent love lives according to their own temperaments, desires, and ambitions. But women born earlier lived in a time when the rules of courtship still governed romantic relations between women and men, young and old. Love almost always meant marriage, and marriage was forever. These options suited many women, who valued and needed their husbands and not infrequently merged their identities with those of the men they married. Even when love seemed to go wrong, they were reluctant to end the relationship. And when they think now of love, they often recall those romantic moments of first meeting, of love renewed even in absence, of love rediscovered after years apart.

Some of the memoirs in this chapter have to do with love in a time of war, and they represent the countless other experiences of women of this generation, separated from those they loved and desperately uncertain of what the future might bring. Others relate the glorious experience of falling in love, or the unexpected passion that is sometimes experienced by those who meet love a second time, or the often imperfect match of expectation and reality. Still others illustrate the loved one's special qualities, and the remembered goodness that lingers after the pain of a final illness.

If these women felt bitterness or betrayal in love, they were unwilling to write about it. Instead, they focused on the recalled events and feelings that gave them pleasure or that best matched their hopes and dreams for love. Even if their lives brought disappointment and loss in love, perhaps the years have burnished and polished the experience so that love still shines in their memory with a gentle and steadfast light.

'Til We Meet Again
Sherlie Hurwitz

It was 1943, and I was one of the many World War II brides who lived in daily apprehension of the dreaded message, "Honey, I'm shipping out."

My message came about a month before our first wedding anniversary. My husband Al was being temporarily reassigned to the Air Force Base in Greensboro, North Carolina, to await orders for his POE (port of embarkation), and dependents were not encouraged to accompany them. However, it was wartime, and my husband and I decided that I would accompany him and stay until someone in authority told me I would have to return home, or he was restricted to the base and unable to be with me. He might not be able to tell me when he was leaving, but we agreed that if he did not call or show up for more than a day, I should assume he had shipped out and return home to Corpus Christi to be with my parents until he returned.

For the second time in less than a year, we went through the next-to-impossible task of finding a temporary place to live, in a city where thousands of wartime couples were homeless while awaiting their next duty assignments. We walked residential streets, knocking on all front doors to inquire if they had a room to rent. It was interesting that no one was shocked or impatient with this query from strangers at their front door—in fact, almost all of them *did* rent rooms in their homes to servicemen, but none seemed to be vacant at the time we were looking. We did have a brief glimmer of hope when someone said, "Yes, I just had a vacancy open up yesterday," and showed us to a very large, bright, well-furnished room. The only problem was that it had four double beds in it, and when we inquired about that, the owner explained that the room was rented to four couples at a time, and one of them had just shipped out the day before. To the question of privacy, she said that they just took turns going to the movies or out to dinner at various times so that each couple had some private time together. Needless to say, we continued on our quest.

Just as we were feeling it was a hopeless venture, we found an upstairs room in the home of a lovely older lady. The only minor flaw was that it was situated about a hundred feet from the railroad tracks, but we felt that was a very insignificant inconvenience for a clean, wonderful room of our own. As it turned out, every day and night troop trains passed the back of the house, and I rushed out on the upstairs back porch to watch them and wonder if my soldier was on the train.

Then one morning, as Al was leaving to go back to the base, he seemed to have a harder time leaving, and came back for one more good-bye kiss and a longer-than-usual hug. About 11 A.M. I heard a train coming and quickly rushed out on the back porch, just in time to see my serviceman leaning out the side window of the train, waving both arms! The train was moving so fast that I couldn't convince myself beyond doubt that it was Al. I waited one more day to be sure he wasn't coming back to the room, and then booked a train home to Corpus Christi.

I didn't know it then, but Al sailed for overseas five days later —the very day I arrived home in Corpus Christi and the day of our first wedding anniversary, May 23, 1944. When I got home, I found a beautiful flower arrangement for our anniversary, with a card in Al's handwriting—too familiar for me to mistake that handwriting! But the most surprising thing was still to come. Every Saturday for the next year, I received a bouquet of flowers, each with a loving card that he had personally signed. He had pre-arranged and paid for this before he shipped out. And the luckiest thing of all was that he returned home from the war safe and sound, for me to spend the rest of my lifetime with!

 Love Letters
Nadeane Walker Anderson

As a *Stars and Stripes* staff writer in Berlin in early 1946, I went to the American Press Club and started dancing with a new arrival, a British war correspondent for the Associated Press who had been a prisoner of war for three and a half years. He brought me earrings made by a friend of his in a new Paris costume jewelry workshop. I put them on, we started to waltz, and I promptly scratched his nose with the spiky earring, so hard that it started to stream with blood. He was dabbing at the scratch with a handkerchief when a red-haired captain, part of the Press Center staff, rushed up and offered to knock his block off, thinking that the bloody nose resulted from my efforts to defend myself from unwanted attention. We disabused him, and went on to a romantic attachment.

I kept all my husband's letters, those written before and after we married. I spent two long vacations in Texas with friends and family when he couldn't come with me, and throughout his working life he was sent on assignment all over the world. I often went with him until our children were born in the mid-fifties, but after that I stayed with them. Whenever we were apart, we wrote to each other every day. I kept his letters, but did not know whether he had kept mine. When I asked him, he made such a noncommittal reply that I thought he had not.

But when I looked in his desk after he died, I found a box labeled "Personal Letters," and there were all my letters to him. I could not have been more pleased if I had found a box of diamonds or gold coins. They, together with his letters to me, are indeed my treasures. They make me laugh and cry when I reread them. There are nearly a hundred letters in each collection. I want our children to read them when I am gone.

Those Golden Days at Graceland
Katherine Koonce

I had looked forward to going to Graceland College in Lamoni, Iowa, for as long as I knew what college was. I remember myself as a child, poring over my mother's scrapbook from her days at Graceland from 1922 to 1924. Her scrapbook contained a fascinating collection of pictures, pressed flowers, notes, cards, and programs from years before. I knew she loved going to Graceland. I was anxious to go there too. When that time came, I wasn't disappointed, and I think of my two years there (1952–1954) as golden ones.

I loved the pretty little campus on a hill. The trees were tall and beautiful, oaks and evergreens, and the lilac bushes saturated the air with their fragrance in the spring. I loved gathering in the student center on Sunday evenings to sing old songs. I loved the small, friendly classes, and I loved the special friendships of the girls' dorm.

On one Sunday night, in September of my freshman year, I met my future husband, Gearl Koonce. I was seventeen years old. Families in the town invited all the new students to attend church service in town and then go in small groups to their homes afterwards for refreshments and a social time. In my group, among others I can't remember, was a girl from Hawaii, Pauline Leiloha, and twins from Texas, Gearl and Earl Koonce. I soon found out that the twins played football, quarterback and halfback, and later I found out that they loved to sing when they sang in a western quartet at a rally at the football field. They sang with their cousin, Fred Church, and a friend, Windy Parker.

Gearl and I began dating. I think he asked me for a date that night or soon afterwards, and by December, I was wearing his high school class ring. It was a wonderful time of discovery and innocence. We had no car, so we would walk the mile—or maybe it was two miles—to town to go to the show, eat pork tenderloin sandwiches, and drink thick milkshakes at the coffee shop in the old hotel. We often played "Up the Lazy River," by the Mills Brothers, on the jukebox there. It was just fun being college kids in love, and sharing the excitement with other young couples.

Sometimes we go back to Graceland Homecoming. We laugh and talk again with old friends who also remember those golden days at Graceland.

How My Life Changed
Amparo González

My life changed dramatically during a seemingly insignificant job as clerk at a hardware store. My brother-in-law managed the hardware and auto supply store in the small town where he and my sister lived. I lived with them for a while and was thankful for the few dollars I earned at the store. The change I'm speaking of was not brought on by the work. It was one of those times when the Holy Spirit places you at the exact location that will change your destiny.

One of my sister's neighbors was fond of saying that she wished her son could meet a small-town girl like me. She told me all about him, and about his Air Force duties. To a country girl, who had never been farther than three hundred miles from home, this fellow's life sounded pretty glamorous.

One day, in walks this handsome guy I had only seen in pictures at his mother's house. It was María's son. She had sent him to the store, I think, for an electrical outlet, but I knew she just wanted us to meet.

How do you know, when you meet someone, that your life will never be the same again? It was sort of magical because, although I was a big girl, I was still waiting for my knight in shining armor. I soon found out that we shared the same values, enjoyed the same things, even loved walking in the rain. We were in love and spent every waking hour together until he had to return to his base. We promised to write often and I was soon getting and answering a letter a day. When he returned in spring, I was in for a surprise. He had a proposal and an engagement ring in hand.

When we talked of getting married, I knew my father would want us to have a big wedding, with a sit-down dinner, as he had done for my sister. I didn't want that, because he was not in good health and I knew he couldn't afford it. It was then that we decided to have a small ceremony. We discussed it with the local priest, a marvelous man, not much older than us, and he approved. My intended and his father then made arrangements to visit our home and ask for my hand in marriage. Then there was a bridal shower, given by my sister and a dear cousin, and finally the trip to buy my trousseau. Because of our limited funds, I decided I would wear a borrowed wedding gown. When the priest gave his homily on our wedding day, the material things, which were lacking, lost their importance. Many who were there said it was one of the most beautiful wedding homilies they had ever heard. Another gift from the Holy Spirit.

There is a postscript to this story. That same priest officiated at our daughter's wedding, thirty-eight years later.

To Do As I Pleased
Minnie Ree Baccus

I remember the day I decided to marry Virgil Alexander. I was eighteen, a junior in high school. My fiancé went to ask my mother and daddy to marry me. My mother said, "Oh, I thought you'd finish school!" and then she cried. I was disappointed because I thought she'd be happy that I was marrying such a nice young man.

My father didn't say a word. My mother did the talking.

I remember Mother did take me shopping. She bought me some pretty nice clothes. My wedding dress was a royal blue dress with a dropped waist. The material was stripes of crepe and satin. The lowered waist was at the hips. It was short, above the knee—well, knee-length. She bought a hat the same color —blue, a blue velvet hat.

I didn't have time to plan a wedding. We were married by the Justice of the Peace. Some people might have thought I was pregnant, but I wasn't. I was just young—maybe too young to know my own mind. We had a honeymoon in a small town (Clinton, Oklahoma) for a couple of nights.

I was very much in love, but another reason I wanted to get married was so I could do as I pleased. I played high school basketball. Our uniforms had bloomers with full-length stockings. The other girls and I rolled our stockings down. That practice stopped for me when my father came to a ball game.

After Virgil and I married, I continued going to school and playing basketball. One night when I went on the bus to a ball game away from our town, Virgil had to work and couldn't go to the game. He decided I should quit basketball, and after that I never got to do as I pleased.

A Keepsake Penny, and Love Refound
Eula Rae McCown

One of my many keepsakes is a penny with a hole shot through it.

It was March 1946 when I began dating Lt. J. Logan Mc-Cown, my future husband. He was stationed in Squadron K at Ellington Air Field, Houston, Texas, and I was the secretary to the Squadron Commander.

We had had a few dates when Mac asked me if I knew of a place where he could do some target practice with his .22 automatic pistol. I was raised in the country, had shotguns, and felt at home with his request. I suggested we go down to Galveston Beach and I would take a picnic lunch and he could safely shoot his pistol.

On Saturday, we drove down to Galveston, East Beach, where we were completely alone. There was not a person in sight.

Mac pushed the heel of his shoe into the sand and placed the penny upright in the footprint. He emptied all of the shots from his clip. (I believe there were eleven bullets.) All he did was flip up the sand and sometimes the penny, but he never hit it.

After watching this sad display of bad marksmanship, I asked if I might shoot the gun. Mac had no sisters, and he was visibly shocked at my suggestion. He reloaded the clip and handed me the gun. The first shot, I hit the penny. He simply could not believe his eyes. He carried that penny in his pocket for years. The instant I hit the penny, I knew I had a husband, if I wanted him.

Now, it is October of 1999, and I got a phone call from a dear friend, telling me that her brother's wife had just died, and asking me (since I knew him from long ago) to send him a card or telephone him.

I have been a widow for ten years. I feel I have made a very happy life for myself. I became Catholic and serve as coordinator of senior adults at the largest Catholic Church in Austin, Texas. All is well with me.

But I did send a card, and then decided to telephone. I was really quite nervous as I heard my friend's brother's voice, so familiar to me fifty-six years ago. We had just begun to talk when he said someone was at the door and he had to hang up the phone. I felt like a dumb wit. But in just a few days he telephoned me back. Then he began to call every night and came to meet me again one month after his wife was buried.

As soon as he walked into my home I closed the door and said, "I want a hug and a kiss." I was shocked by the emotions I felt. I had been known to say quite often, "I do not want some wrinkled old man kissing me on the lips!" and here I had invited a wrinkled old man to kiss me. We were both shocked by our feelings. When we parted from the kiss and hug, I took his hands and said, "I have to say a prayer. You see, I am a minister and I pray a lot and you will have to accept that as a regular part of my life."

My friend is very religious and active in his church. I love this about him, for I could not love someone who was not religious. We have both found love again and are shocked at how much more intense the feelings are today than they were when we were married to other people before. My beloved now telephones me to wake me up each morning (quite a bit nicer than the alarm clock). He calls again before I go to work; he calls during my lunch hour when I am home for lunch. We speak when I get home from work and then again in the evening. His phone bill is terrible, but he says it is worth it. I feel marriage is in the future, but I live in Austin and he lives in Houston. We pray for God to lead us and tell us what to do, but so far God is very quiet.

I have shared the story with all of my widow friends and I know this gives them hope, for none of us know what the future holds.

"Hey, Maud Farkle . . ."
Paula Stephens-Bishop

Bill Stephens was my first love—my soul mate, if there is such a thing. He wasn't movie-star handsome, but he was the best-looking hunk I'd ever seen. I knew the first time I saw him that we'd marry.

I remember one Sunday afternoon, when we went to the motorcycle races. I intended to race in the women's powder-puff division. My husband would race in the men's tag-team. Favored by everyone to win, I might as well have been ten feet tall and bulletproof. The judges' instructions were to race to the flagman, turn back into the riverbed, and then race for the finish line.

I grinned as I revved my Bultaco, tightened my helmet, and told my friend and riding partner, "Nothing to it. A piece of cake. Shouldn't take over fifteen minutes." The flag went down, and I was off in the lead. For several minutes I heard the clamor and clatter of a dozen or so motorcycles, then only my buddy's and mine. As I zipped up hills and struggled down gullies, I searched for the flagman.

An hour later, as I rode over terrain so rough that even I, a daredevil, found difficult to maneuver, I ceased hearing my buddy's motor. Moments later, I saw a group of Boy Scouts, and Lake Meredith. There was no way I was going to turn back into the riverbed—it was a full-fledged body of water. I stopped to rest, and Bill caught up with me. He'd caught my buddy a few miles earlier and turned her back. The flagman hadn't been in position. We were thirty miles or so from the finish line. Need-less to say, I didn't win the race.

Bill's most endearing trait was his patience—not only with me, but with everyone he was in contact with. I'm sure he had an annoying trait, but when you lose someone, you tend to for-get the little things that drove you crazy. What makes me the happiest when I think of him is the fun we shared with our chil-dren and our granddaughters. What makes me the saddest is that our grandson Travis was born three years after Bill died. He will never know the love of his grandfather.

What do I remember best? The list is endless. I still close my eyes and smell his after-shave lotion. I listen close and hear him sing his favorite song, "I'll Fly Away." I feel his arms around me when I remember how we danced. When I'm desperate, I hear him say, "Hey, Maud Farkle, things could be worse . . ."

Do You Believe in Fate?
Evelyn Simon

Do you believe in fate? I certainly do. Think back about events that occurred in your life. If you had not been in a certain place at a certain time, or had not met a certain person, would your life be different? My destiny occurred in the fourth grade when I met the boy who would later become my husband. You see, I would never have met him had he not been in an automobile accident when he was in the first grade at the parochial school, and had to sit out a year.

Because of all the things I was allergic to around the school, I was sent to the public school near my home for second and third grades. My husband's family moved to New Orleans, where he attended second and third grades. They moved back as he began fourth grade at the parochial school.

It was decided that enough time had passed that perhaps I could overcome my allergies, and I was sent back to parochial school for the fourth grade. However, because of crowded classrooms, all the students who were not there the prior year were put in a special class that was combined with like third graders. The nun taught the two grades in one room, which is another story entirely. I remember trading school pictures and running home to show my mom his picture.

"That's the boy I will marry," I announced. She looked at the picture and said, "Oh sure, well, I guess he's cute enough." Never in her wildest dreams did she think I would ever marry him! She should have realized how persistent I could be when I wanted something.

Do you think it was destiny? I know we would never have met had he not had the accident, as our school only went up to eighth grade and then you went on to the public high school. Being a grade ahead of me, he would have gone on to public school and I would never have seen him again. We lived five miles apart, and our paths would never have crossed. And had I not had asthma and stayed in the public school near my house, I would have been in the other fourth-grade class and never really would have gotten to know him.

Yes, I believe in fate!

"I Will Promise You a Rose Garden"
Val Jean Schmidt

"I will promise you a rose garden if you'll marry me."

I had met this New Yorker, who didn't like Mexican food, two years before at a Christmas party. On Christmas Eve, 1978, I became Mrs. Harry C. Schmidt. He kept his promise.

We managed to work around most of our differences. After convincing Harry that I went into withdrawal if I didn't get Mexican food at least every three weeks, he learned to eat tacos and fajitas. I learned to make New York cheesecake. Before this, mine had a graham cracker crust. (Actually, I got Lindy's famous recipe from a teacher who had been friends with Lindy's *maître d'*. This was almost like divine intervention.)

One of Harry's greatest joys was planning our next trip—Christmas, spring break, summer vacation. What wonderful trips they were because of his thorough plans.

In June 1991 I retired from teaching, and that October we went on our long-awaited fall foliage trip to New England, Nova Scotia, and Prince Edward Island. When we returned, we celebrated Thanksgiving, then the following Saturday we picked out and brought home our live Christmas tree—a must for Harry. That night we went to see the movie *Cape Fear*. At bedtime, Harry was setting the alarm clock, for we were to prepare Communion for church the next morning. I heard a thud, and found him on the floor. He had suffered a massive stroke. In a second, both our lives were forever changed.

After the hospital, rehab, and many therapists, he remained paralyzed on his left side—face, arm, and leg. However, he could stand and pivot. This made it possible for me to care for him in our home. He was changed, but much of the old personality remained.

On August 6, 1998, I lost this wonderful guy. I was blessed to have him for almost twenty years.

CHAPTER SIX

Loss

The Strength to Survive

Nothing can avert the inevitability of loss.

Some kind of loss comes with every change we encounter through the years of our lives. Moving from one home to another, from one job or one marriage to another, illness, death, separation—all these changes entail the loss of familiar surroundings, of comfortable habits, of long-accepted understandings. Adding to the cost, change often dissolves long-standing bonds of friendship and community.

Our physical capacities also change with age. Strength and endurance deteriorate. Vision and hearing decline and may entirely fail. The physiological processes of aging can steal memory and with it, identity. Youthful beauty fades, a special worry to women who have accepted the cultural judgment that appearance is a standard of worth. And although idealism and optimism may survive, a certain loss of innocence is inevitable as we attempt to match our hopes against the reality of life. As people grow older and confront time's limitations, many grieve their unrealized dreams and expectations.

According to psychologists, writing about loss helps us to understand it, clarify our feelings, and gain some perspective. As these older women wrote about their losses, it was also clear that the writing took courage, for loss is painful, and facing it honestly and openly is not an easy or comfortable thing to do.

"This is hard work," many of the writers said. "It hurts to remember this." But they stayed with it, finding something valuable even among their losses.

"Writing helps," one woman said gratefully, when she had finished. "It helps a *lot*."

It does.

The Lost Shoes
Alice M. Short

It was the summer of 1944. My mother, my two sisters, and I went downtown to our doctor's office. My youngest sister needed to see the doctor, but we all had to go. After the doctor's visit, we went to the shoe repair store to pick up two pairs of shoes that had been reheeled or resoled, or maybe both. Then we were going shopping for a very few essentials we needed at Grants. It had a basement, and I remember vividly walking down the stairs and going directly to the department where they sold little girls' jewelry. It was so much fun looking at it all. Naturally, the shoes I was carrying were put down in order for me to look at the jewelry. A few minutes later my mother had finished her shopping and said, "Alice, let's go, we want to catch the next bus."

As we were walking out of the store, I remembered the shoes. I ran back downstairs where I had been, but they were gone. We walked all over the store and went to the office to ask if anyone had turned in a package. Tears welled up in my mother's eyes and I cried, but we did not find the shoes. I was so devastated about this event that I do not know who did without the shoes. How I wish my mother was alive today so that I could ask her.

The Day My Childhood Died
Ruby Varnon Bishop

I grew up in a very close-knit family, but my mother began to show serious signs of mental illness when I was around five years old. My early remembrance was of a fun-loving person who sang and drew pictures. As the illness progressed, she changed into a moody, violent individual. I lost a loving parent and I began to live in fear of the violent times.

In the years until I was about nine, Mother was in and out of a sanitarium, located in Oklahoma. In these years, she would spend no more than two or three months at a time with us. She would have to be sent back to the sanitarium. This was a very unsettling time for me. When she was at home, she was not the fun-loving person I remembered, but was easily angered and was violent.

Once, I remember, it had been raining, and a car slid off the road and into a ditch. The man was stuck in knee-deep mud. As children, my brother and I thought this was funny. We were standing at the dining room window watching the man as he tried to get his car from the ditch. We were laughing, and this angered my mother. She came into the room with a boning knife in her hand and came toward me. I knew I was going to be hit. I put my hand up over my eyes, and she cut the outer part of my hand to the bone. After it happened, she sat down and cried. She was very remorseful for her actions. The serenity of my childhood was shattered, and much of the time I lived in fear. My brother and I never told our father about these violent outbreaks until many years later.

Mother was diagnosed as paranoid schizophrenic when I was nine. The doctor told my father that she needed to be declared mentally insane in the courts, and sent to the State Mental Hospital in Wichita Falls. This was an extremely agonizing time for my father. I never saw him cry much in my life, but during this time he cried many times. The ladies from the church came and stayed around the clock with us, while the paper process was going through and a schedule was being set to have the mental health people come to our home and pick up my mother. She would wander through the house and talk to people who were not there. She would not eat and very seldom slept.

Many times Mom would do what I requested, when she would refuse anyone else. I remember my father asking me to see if I could get her to eat. She did sit down at the table, and I placed a bowl of soup in front of her and took one for myself. We were alone, as any other person in the room made her fly into a rage. I remember as if it was yesterday. She looked at me, smiled, picked up the bowl, and threw the hot soup in my face. The burn was bad, but what really hurt was her railing about me trying to poison her.

The next day, the mental health people were scheduled to pick her up at 8 A.M. By nine, they had not arrived, and my father went to my grandparents' house to call. He left us with my mother and the ladies from the church. He was gone only a few minutes when they arrived. No child should witness what my brother and I saw then. She fought, kicked, scratched, pulled hair, screamed, and cried. They finally had her on the floor and got her into a straitjacket. At this time she began to beg and cry for my brother and me to help her. My childhood died that day, and I was never the same.

My brother and I have dealt with this mental illness all of our lives. You see, Mom is eighty-seven, and only three months ago we had her back in the hospital. Mom was lost to us years ago, but her life has left a terrible ache for things that might have been.

When Daddy Died
Ruby A. Taylor

Paul W. Walker, fifty-six, Waco grocer, was discovered by his wife dead in a garage at the rear of his home at 1601 Park Avenue with a bullet wound in his head at 8:20 A.M. Monday. He owned and operated a store and market at 816 N. 27th St. On the floor near his body was a .38-caliber Colt pistol with one chamber empty. At the inquest a verdict of death from gunshot wounds, self-inflicted, was rendered.

Mother, with three small children to rear, went to court and proved my father's death was accidental. The insurance company wouldn't pay Daddy's insurance with a verdict of self-inflicted wounds. More than the money, she wanted to clear his name. I still have the telegram, dated January 21, 1928, which reads, "We won the case. Daddy's name is clear. Will be home Sunday. Annie 3:35 P.M." I also have the yellowed clipping with the headline, "P. W. Walker Dead by His Own Hand."

There is so much more to this story. In 1927, in Waco, Texas, there was a rash of killings. Men who went to work early were targeted. When a car stopped for a light, this madman jumped on the running board and shot point blank at the driver. Several were killed, but one who lived said it was a black man. He was later caught, but he is why my Daddy died. Daddy bought a gun, and each morning he put it on the seat of the car beside him. At night he kept it on a high closet shelf. On the day he died, he had the gun in his hand as he walked across our back-yard and up to the small door to the garage. He often brought a barrel of leftover vegetables home for the chickens. This barrel was up against the door. How it got there nobody knew. We children could have rolled it around and it ended up blocking the garage door. As Daddy walked in the dark yard, up to the door, the barrel was about knee high. He fell over it, dragging the toes of his shoes over the barrel as he fell inside the garage. His hand came up and the gun went off, striking him through his glasses. Those were the points that helped prove it was an accident.

My memory begins in our front yard. My brother Weber, who was seven, left for school. Mother, Romell, and I were working and playing when Mother saw that the garage doors were still closed. She didn't worry, as sometimes the car wouldn't start, or the doors blew shut after he left, but she went back to prop them open. I remember her screams, and she ran back to us and grabbed me and rocked me back and forth, still screaming. That's all I remember as neighbors came running and took my sister and me away. No one heard the shot, not Mother or any neighbors. We children were two and a half, five, and seven.

The Strength to Survive
Sarah Lichtman

My mother was together with me in the concentration camp in Ravensbrück, and then in Bergen-Belsen. My mother had typhus in the ghetto, and she was fragile and very weak. I took very hard work in the camp because of my mother. I worked with another person like a horse. We hauled barrels on our shoulders and had to walk miles to pick up the vegetables by hand. They didn't have refrigeration. The work was very hard, but I had a good Nazi woman who turned her head in another direction and you could steal a carrot or a potato and also eat them. The problem was to bring them back to the camp and exchange for bread with Polish women.

As long as I was in Ravensbrück, I tried to take care of my mother. In February of 1945, they transferred us to another camp. Older women were not working. Since my mother was about fifty, she was old, and in the room with women who were scheduled to die. I went with my mother. Then, later, we found out that nobody was working. The days passed, and there was no food, no water, no hope. My mother begged me to go out and find something. I was lucky to find a dress and I offered it to a Ukrainian woman and she gave me a big bag of beets. That kept us going until April 7, when the English freed the camp.

The war was still going on at the Russian front, and the English didn't have too much food, so they gave us the rations that the soldiers were eating. I went to the woods to make some coffee for my mother. I made the coffee and broth and took it back to her. She took one sip and died in my lap. For a day, I couldn't part with my mother and didn't accept her being dead. When she was taken from me, I thought my whole world fell apart.

After the liberation, I thought that I survived the war because of my mother. I was responsible for her welfare, and that gave me strength to survive. Now, when I look around my kitchen—at the dishwasher, the washing machine—I think, what a pity that she couldn't see this, especially since my father survived, and they could have lived together in happiness. When I open my closet, I feel guilty—too many clothes. But I appreciate what I have, and taking care of my mother gave me strength to survive.

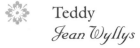

Teddy
Jean Wyllys

I've never told this story before, though most of my friends know I had a brother who was killed in the war. Actually, Teddy never got to the war. But he did, if only briefly, find his heart's desire.

Teddy was seven years older than I was, which is a big gap when you are a child, and I adored him. Most of the time, he ignored me, and that seemed normal. At mealtimes he was very funny, and I still remember his jokes. He was a server in St. Andrew's Church, and I remember him as very devout. He was very good with his hands and loved working with his fret saw: he made a model in plywood of a royal coach used in the coronation of King Edward VIII. Sprayed with gold paint, it captured my heart. I thought he could do anything. When he left school, he started work in a local bank, though his heart's desire was to be an airplane pilot, and when he was old enough, he signed up for the Royal Air Force. I have a photograph of him in his cadet's uniform, looking very young and brave. (At the time, priority was given by photographers to men who were leaving for active duty. Only later did I understand the chilling reality of that.) The cadet pilots were sent to South Africa for their training. I don't remember much about this time, though I have an elephant-hair bracelet he sent in a family gift package.

I do remember the summer day the telegram came to say he had been killed "in an air accident." I think we learned later that it had been his first solo flight, and I've thought so often about what he must have thought at the moment of the crash. On reading the telegram, my mother said immediately: "Now, nobody must know about this—don't tell a soul." Of course, soon everybody knew about it. I think she was just trying to ward off all the inevitable things that did in fact happen: the stream of visitors, the mourning, the closed blinds, the looks people gave us. Most families had someone in one of the services, and what had happened to our family was what everyone was hoping wouldn't happen to them.

My sister Dorothy was sent to tell our father at his office. He came home and hugged us all. It was a strange time. In the days that followed, Dorothy and I stayed in the back of the house so we wouldn't have to deal with the visitors. The front of the house was dark because all the blinds were drawn. There was a funeral, but it was somehow assumed that Dorothy and I would not go, and we were left at home with some busy work. I didn't know how to deal with the situation. I didn't know how I was supposed to act or what I was supposed to say, though someone always let me know if I did or said something inappropriate—that's how I learned. Only once did I try to address the mystery of death with my mother, but she didn't seem to want to talk with me about it.

My brother was buried in what was then Rhodesia, and I have always been ambivalent about whether I should go there one day to honor his memory, or whether I shouldn't. After all, it's only a body buried there. He was nineteen when he died.

Changing Places
Joyce A. Dehlin

Our move to Texas and Sun City was a traumatic experience. Never mind that everyone else moving here had also known change and loss: my grief was strong and deep.

We lived in Minot, North Dakota, for forty-some years. It is a small state, and we knew people from Fargo to Beach. Roots were deep in our church, the community, and our neighborhood, and knowing four generations of a family was not uncommon. Our doctors, dentists, service people were real friends, and each of them was usually available the day that you needed them. We all came to depend upon each other, we supported each other, rejoicing and grieving and growing with each other.

We ordered our house in February and came to Texas in August. When we drove up to our house in the development, it looked like a war zone of construction. All the trees on our lot were gone, and the promised level lot had a steep driveway. The carefully-arranged-for doggy door had not been installed as planned.

We were bewildered and overwhelmed by the changes. We did not know at that time that we could have declined to close on the house. Oh, if only we knew then what we know now! Did these folks have no pride in their workmanship? The quality of the construction was much less perfect than what we had been led to expect from the appearance of the model homes. Foolishly, we trusted the company to carry out all the promises made at sale time. We had visited several friends at other retirement communities, and they all seemed so pleased, so we never doubted that this one would be equally satisfactory.

It seemed that surly customer service people were trained to say "No" to many of the items we wanted corrected. Stores and services were hard to find. We had difficulty (and sometimes still do) finding our way around in Austin. Street names had an interesting way of changing at whim or a highway would have several names. It was confusing to locate businesses in the rush of traffic.

Unlike many Sun City residents who have moved often and have adjusted successfully to new cities and towns, we had not had much practice with such changes. This move was a real struggle. We felt the loss of friendships of long standing, our church friends, work friends, neighbors. We had been very involved in the community and still miss events such as the Scandinavian Festival called the Hostfest, community concerts, Arts in the Park, and New Year's Eve at the country club.

Shortly after we arrived, we went to a dinner at the Social

Center. There must have been four hundred people there, and we did not know one soul! It was difficult after living in a community where we knew and loved so many people. The house is a bit smaller than we thought it would be, therefore, we have had to part with some dear pieces. Also, we feel a little crowded when families come to visit.

So, what do I do with all this? Are we sorry we came here? No! The reason for moving was very strong: to be near our young families and the precious grandchildren. That has been wonderful! We see them more often, and all six of the grands were here for camp last summer. It was a great time. A plus that was not a part of our decision is the warmer weather. I remember standing at the back door in Minot, working to unlock the door with hands stiff with the cold. As we have grown more mature in years, coping with the ice and snow had become more difficult. We have not met anyone we do not like! We have met and become friends with some marvelous people, folks who are warm and kind and helpful. We have found a church home.

People ask me, "How do you like being a Texan?" or "How do you like the Hill Country?" I am always ambivalent. My task is to develop a more contented heart. I'm working at it. Now there are many people and things I would not want to give up here! Be content. Pray for peace of soul. Concentrate on blessings—there are many! Enjoy today.

I feel some guilt for being childish and immature, for not coping better with what others might regard as a trivial concern, but to me it was a trauma. The pain has been real. It is better now. I hope it will continue to improve. I'm working on it.

Renee
Irene Luedke

Renee was the victim of divorce. In fact, she was the victim of a troubled marriage and unplanned pregnancy. Our home was fraught with uncertainties and fear. Her birth interrupted my graduate studies and the attainment of some measure of financial independence for my children and me.

I struggled to hold the marriage together until Renee was twelve years old. I had a teaching position in the public schools now and filed for divorce. Both boys were gone from the home. Renee did her best to take care of both her mother and her father. This child felt responsible for our problems and became sullen and withdrawn. Her life was out of control. Her pre-teen need for separation from Mother in order to become the beautiful functional adult woman she was meant to be was particularly painful for both of us in this setting.

The divorce was final in December 1981. The next year and a half were a nightmare. She was not coping with the situation well at all. She and I had counseling sessions together and apart. We attended Al-Anon and Alateen groups.

She left my home at Christmastime following her fourteenth birthday to live with her father. On my bed she left her Alateen book and a brief note: "Dad needs me, you don't." I have managed only a few brief contacts with her since that time. My heartbreak overwhelms me at times, but hope for reconciliation persists.

 The Day Grandma Died, August 9, 1938
Sidna Leavenworth

I had seen my dog run over by Uncle Jim and die; my parakeet asphyxiated by Quick Henry the Flit, when my brother sprayed him; and my pet dove eaten by the cat—but never had I seen a person die.

A hot summer day in August 1938, Mama sent me down the hill, over the bridge, to get a bottle of Grade A raw milk for breakfast before 7 A.M. Grandma was reading her Bible in the swing on the screened-in porch under the shade of the giant old oak trees, waiting for Papa (my grandpa) to come up from the barn for breakfast. She said what she always said when I ran off over the creek, across the bridge, up the small gravel drive to the big road. "Sidna, watch out for cars and stay on the side of the road. And don't drop the milk bottle."

Shortly after breakfast, the phone rang and Papa was screaming, "Glad, come quick, something's wrong with Maggie." Mama grabbed my two-year-old brother and we three jumped in the old Chevy and raced madly down the road, over the bridge, and up to the house. Mama sent me to the barn to play, and I don't know who took my baby brother. I spent most of the day in the barn, watching the calf being born and cleaned up by its mother. I went to the house in the late afternoon because I was hungry.

Grandma was lying on the bed. Papa was weeping, and Mama was rubbing Grandma's feet. The doctor came and said, "There's no use taking her to town to the hospital. She'll be dead by sunset," and she was. I went back to the barn and stroked the now-dry calf, standing wobbly by its mam, trying to nurse, and I thought my Grandma was alive in the calf's body. I had never heard of reincarnation, but that's what I thought.

Six months later, Papa married Trudy, Grandma's cousin from East Texas who was a known abortionist, according to Mama, and I was told never to go down the hill and cross over the bridge again. I personally thought, at age eight, that Trudy was much better suited for Papa than Grandma had been. But what does a kid know?

"I Should Have Cried"
Lucy A. Boyea

Daddy was sixty-nine years of age when I was born. My mother was thirty-two years his junior. I was the youngest of four children, having three older brothers, although my third brother died in infancy, so I never knew him.

Daddy was an architect by profession, but retired when I was less than a year old. My mother, a registered nurse, worked outside the home, so my father was my primary caretaker. He was a handsome six-footer, with white hair, a white mustache, and blue eyes. He was the epitome of dignity. We were inseparable, because although he had two sons, I was the proverbial apple of his eye.

I don't recall any annoying traits, but certainly one of my most endearing memories is of Daddy putting me to bed, listening to the call of a whippoorwill and singing "The Long, Long Trail." Daddy taught me an appreciation of nature (we lived on a twenty-two-acre farm in New Hampshire): where to find wild strawberries and jack-in-the-pulpits, how to tap maple trees, and how creative one could be with snow.

As time went by, Daddy's health became a source of concern, and my brothers and I were very protective of him, opening the garage door when my mother came home from work so he would not have to do it. Daddy died very suddenly with a massive coronary when I was eight years old. We were living in New Hampshire at the time, but he was buried in New Haven, Connecticut, which necessitated two funeral services. I distinctly remember that I should have cried, but found it impossible to do. I also refused to touch him following his death. (My mother kissed him as he lay in his coffin.)

In years following my father's death, certain floral scents immediately reminded me of Daddy's funeral. My regret at the loss of my father at such an early age is offset by the many happy memories I have of him, as well as the fact that I was blessed with a wonderful mother.

❀ Losing Martha
Bobbye Jo Barker

When I look back to my childhood, those years seem to be fraught with difficult and unhappy times. How much of that is how it really was, or how much the memories are the faulty perceptions of a child, I will never know. I do know that my sister

Martha was the one I was close to. She was the lively, spirited one of the family, the one I could talk to, and the one who listened and understood. There were three girls in the family. I was the youngest. Martha was the middle child. We fought a lot as children, but time and a little maturity changed that and drew us even closer, especially after Martha became ill.

Martha married a naval officer during World War II. After the war, her husband was sent to Washington, D.C. They had a daughter eighteen months old by that time. Martha missed her family in Dallas, but commented that at least she wouldn't have to worry about her little girl contracting polio, which reached epidemic proportions every hot summer in Texas. This was 1948, twelve years before the Salk vaccine.

Washington had relatively few cases of polio that August. Ironically, both Martha and her daughter Tanis were stricken with the disease. Martha's condition worsened to the point she had to be placed in an iron lung. Tanis recovered without any ill effects. Martha was finally able to leave the respirator and lived ten more years, though she was almost completely paralyzed. She died on Christmas Eve, 1957. She was thirty-three years old.

Loving and missing Martha does not seem to diminish with the years. As I try and recall stories from the past, I especially wish she were here to see if my memories match her recollections. I miss our long talks, her sense of humor, laughing together when she had every reason to cry. She died too young, but she was such a blessing while she lived.

When I Think of Grace . . .
Jeanie Forsyth

When I think of grace, what immediately leaps to mind? My daughter Nancy and the last two weeks of her life. She lived them with unusual and unexpected grace and courage.

When I first arrived at her bedside in Alexandria Hospital in early August 1998, before the Denver shunt began to drain the fluid from her lungs, she was not getting enough oxygen to her brain, was confused and hallucinating, paranoid. She saw water on the floor that wasn't there, and thought the nurses and doctors were in a conspiracy against her. I was alarmed by her appearance, her body so wasted in the year since I had last seen her. There was still a question of whether to do chemotherapy, not in the hope of a cure (the cancer was already in the chest wall), but perhaps to prolong her life an extra month or two. But she had to participate in the decision. In answer to my question "What would you do if it were you?" her oncologist, a compassionate man, told me, "I would choose not to have treatment."

In the next days she was lucid most of the time. We talked. There was the option of hospice, the hope of two or three more months of life. It seemed to me futile and unnecessarily cruel to go through the suffering chemotherapy would cause. Nancy agreed. There were still some periods of confusion. Once, she said, "I wish I knew what was happening to me."

I told her as gently as I could. "Nancy, the cancer has come back, and it can't be treated. We're just going to do all we can to keep you comfortable." And I told her I would stay with her from that moment on. It was then, that moment, that the element of grace entered. She said to me, "I guess that means I won't get to see the year 2000, and I'll never get to go to Europe." That was the last mention she made of any regret.

From that moment she lived in the present, was able to appreciate—and express her appreciation to—her wonderful caregivers, and charmed them all. She healed a longtime rift with her second brother, had long talks with her other two brothers, and could say to me, "I'm glad I've had this time with you. It's one of the best times we've had together." And another time, she said, "There's three people here: you, me, and you-me, y'know?" I did know.

She kept her sense of humor. Four days before she died she said, "This is really wicked fun: living in my bed and having everything done for me."

So, what does *grace* mean to me? A certain elegance or

beauty of action, a willingness to accept and acquiesce to what is, without complaint, as terribly unfair and out of order as it may be, to make a gift of time and memory to those one loves. Where does it come from? From whatever divine spark there is deep within, which for Nancy caught fire and burned brightly those last two weeks.

CHAPTER SEVEN

Living Fully

I Still Had My Two Dollars

When the women of the OWL Circle Project write about their lives, they write about an amazing variety of remembered experiences, the fruit of long, full lives, fully lived. Money may have been hard to come by when they were growing up, but most feel they are living in better times and greater financial security. They may have lacked some creature comforts—electricity, running water, an automatic washer—but they recall work done with honest satisfaction. Entertainment may have been a trip to the movies once a month or a forty-nine-cent Nancy Drew mystery bought with a week's pay, but they had fun, they celebrated often, and they remember it all with pleasure. "Times were simpler then," one woman said, "but we got more out of the simple things. They meant more, somehow." And when they wrote about what had made them happy, it was, indeed, the simple things: summer and roller skates, two dollars to buy honey and tortillas, the Red Sox, a red convertible, and a ride on an elephant.

Full living can also mean adventures of all sorts: going on a camping trip in the Big Bend, seeing the first steps of a little polio survivor, becoming a college queen candidate, going to the Saturday matinee. "We write to taste life twice," Anaïs Nin has said. And when life tastes like a day at the ball game with Dad, or the publication of a first poem, or pretend-wine shared with Grandma, the writing and the recollection are all the more satisfying.

Decoration Day, Fairy Tales, and the Ice Cream Wagon
Oma Gillis

May 30 was a national holiday known as Decoration Day. It was always celebrated on May 30, regardless of the day it occurred, and not over the nearest weekend. There was always a parade, not spectacular as many are today, but the townspeople gathered to watch, lining the main street. The local band led the parade. A few floats, decorated with the flowers in bloom— lilacs, snowballs, peonies, iris, and a few early-blooming roses —followed. Veterans of the Civil War, now quite old and fewer each year, rode in the open touring cars, followed by Spanish-American veterans marching. The flowers were later taken to the cemetery.

In the late afternoon many families brought blankets and picnic baskets to the town square for the band concert, which was held in the bandstand in the center. School ended a day or so after Decoration Day, and always started again the day after Labor Day.

Even though you really enjoyed going to school, the summer holidays were a wonderful time to enjoy lazy, hazy days with long evenings. After I had put my bedroom in passable order, helped wash or dry the dishes, possibly pulled a few weeds in the garden, and practiced my piano lesson, the day was free for me to enjoy. I read a great deal, and almost every day I made a trip to the library to return the book I had completed and to take home another. One summer, I remember I read books of fairy tales: *The Pink Book of Fairy Tales, The Blue Book of Fairy Tales,* all the way through a great number of colors.

I either walked or roller-skated to the library, a distance of about five blocks. I spent a lot of time on roller skates, and had scuffed knees and elbows all summer. There were three or four children my age in the neighborhood, and we all collected at one home or another to play games. Croquet was one of the favorites. We had a croquet set in place on one side of the house that was only taken down to mow the grass. The grownups played after dinner in the evening, but the children played in the daytime. The only rule was that the mallets and balls were to be returned to the box when we finished playing.

We also played games like "Run Sheep Run." One of my favorites that probably today's children have never heard of was called "Statue." One child was designated the swinger. In turn, she would take the hand of another and they would whirl and turn. When released, you were supposed to stumble a few feet, landing in a position where you froze and became a statue. We all vied to see who could assume the most beautiful and artistic pose and hold it. Sometimes we varied it by attempting to be the most grotesque.

When my sister was three, after she had had her nap one afternoon, my mother dressed her and took her down to the sandbox in the backyard to play. My mother fastened a lightweight clothesline around Mary's waist and tied the other end to a nearby tree branch. Sometime later in the afternoon, a friend of my mother's who lived about four blocks away telephoned her and inquired, "Do you know where Mary is?" When my mother replied that she was playing in the sandbox, her friend said, "I think you had better check. I'm sure she is up here, and she doesn't have on a stitch of clothing!" After that, baby-watching was added to my responsibilities.

In the middle of the afternoon, the ice cream wagon, a cart drawn by horses, would come down our street, announcing its approach by a jangling bell. We all rushed out with our nickels to buy an ice cream cone. At dusk in the evening we chased fireflies and imprisoned them in small jars. It seemed as if summer had only arrived when Labor Day heralded the return of school days.

✿ I Still Had My Two Dollars
Marji Smith

There have been times in my life when money was in short supply. During those times, the money we did have was spent with a little more thought about what we really needed, as opposed to what we *wanted*.

One time, my husband and I had maybe three dollars between his paychecks. We lived in a tiny town outside of Austin and had two dogs, Trudy and Jason. Jason was just a puppy. A large truck came down the road at a high rate of speed, and of course, the dog was at the edge of the road. I heard a yelp and saw Jason running under the house. I crawled under the house, since he wouldn't come out, and dragged him out. His leg was pretty cut up.

So here I am, no gas in the car, no money for a vet bill, and an injured puppy. I put the dog in the car, grabbed my three dollars and took off for the next town, which was eight miles away. I put a dollar's worth of gas in the car, so now I had two dollars to use as a down payment on the vet bill.

When I got to the vet's office, no one was there. The door was unlocked, so I went in. They were surprised to see me inside when they got there for work. I told them what had happened and that I only had two dollars cash, and asked if there was a payment plan I could use.

As it turned out, they let me clean the vet's office as a trade for stitching up the dog's leg. I still had my two dollars, so I bought flour tortillas and honey, enough to last two days.

Baseball Fever
Jane R. Peppard

My dad and I had season tickets to the Boston Red Sox. We started going to the games in 1945, when I was twelve. Dad was able to scrape up enough money in 1946, and we got tickets for every holiday and every Sunday home game. It was a great treat.

Baseball had suffered from an acute manpower shortage during World War II, as did all businesses and industries. Nonetheless, in those years, my dad and I became very close. Dad introduced me to my very first Stevens concession hot dog at a 1945 baseball game at Fenway Park. Nothing ever since has tasted so good.

We would go to the game at 10 A.M. and watch batting practice until the game started at 2 P.M. The greatest thrill was to see Ted Williams step up to the batters' box to take his licks. He hit many a ball out of the park. We brown-bagged our lunch to save money. The entire day was very long. After the game was over, we waited for the players to shower. Then, when they were all cleaned up and their hair was slicked down, we waited at the parking lot gate to get their autographs. They were just so happy that we waited for them and requested their autographs.

Dad tried to teach me how to score the game on the scorecard. As much as I loved the game, I never really mastered the method. I think it was because committing the play to paper meant taking my eye off the ball and missing the next play—it was just too distracting.

At some early-season games in April, we were so cold that we had to stuff newspapers into our clothing and down our backs to insulate ourselves against that cold Boston northeast wind.

Later, my mom became a fan, just to be able to participate in our conversations. She and I would go to Ladies' Day for fifteen cents admission—we had so much fun. We, too, took our lunch, as we also went at 10 A.M. to watch batting practice and fielding practice. Afterward, we had to hurry home to make dinner for Dad. We always rehashed the game for him, so he felt that he had not missed anything.

I became a baseball trivia nut and knew lots of statistics. Before the baseball games, there was a live quiz program broadcast on radio station WHDH from Fenway Park. The program was called Jerry O'Leary's Baseball Quiz. I entered the contest twice, and won the grand prize each time—ten silver dollars.

I saved those precious programs and scorecards, all rolled up, curled up, and creased and stuck together with sweat and signed by my heroes: Ted Williams, Bobby Doerr, Johnny Pesky, Dave

"Boo" Ferris, and Tex Hughson, my mother's idol. My Dad loved Ted. We met the same fans week after week, year after year, as we all had the same seats—we became a "baseball family." We stayed in touch with each other until 1952, when I went off to nursing school. Then it was all work, no time or money for tickets. But I followed the games on the radio and in the newspapers, and talked baseball with all my male patients.

I was thrilled to see Ted Williams elected to the All-Century Team and to see him throw out the first pitch at Fenway Park in July 1999 for the All-Star Game. I had seen him play in the 1946 All-Star Game at Fenway Park. What a great day he had, hitting two home runs! This July, he had to be helped out of his wheelchair to throw out the first pitch. Nonetheless, the standing ovation given him by the Boston fans was even louder this year than in 1946. What a hero!

The Best Christmas
Mary G. Warren

The best Christmas I ever had as a child was the year I got my Sonja Henie doll. I think it was 1939 or 1940, and I didn't play with dolls. I'd never even wanted a doll. But Sonja Henie was my very favorite movie star. She was a famous ice skater, but this doll was on skis and she had on beautiful ski clothes and a precious wool cap, with her blond curls showing under the hat. I so wanted this doll. Christmas morning we got up, went to the tree, and there she was: the most beautiful thing I had ever seen.

As I picked her up, my daddy called me over to the front door, and as he opened the door, said, "Look." The ground was covered with snow! It was the first white Christmas I'd ever experienced. I screamed with delight and tried to run out. My mother had brought boots and a coat for me to put on before they let us out. Sonja and I rushed out; I sat her down on the snow. That may have been the happiest moment of my young life. I remember that glorious feeling to this day. God made Big Spring's first and only white Christmas just because I got my Sonja Henie doll.

❁ Inside a Prism
Ruby Varnon Bishop

One year around Christmas holidays, Malcolm, my youngest son, and I traveled to the Panhandle to visit Paula and Bill Stephens. Outside of Fort Worth a light snow began to fall. This made driving very hazardous, but we made the trip without any mishap.

I was to sleep in a room that had double French doors that led to the hot tub area. The hot tub was in a glass atrium. That night before we went to bed, Paula and I had sat up late in the hot tub and watched the snow fall and melt as it hit the glass roof.

As I awoke the next morning, it was as if I was inside a prism. The water on the atrium had frozen into an ice sheet and was being reflected by the sunlight into my bedroom. This was a very special, quite peaceful time, as I lay there looking in wonder at the beautiful colors.

❁ My Bonneville Convertible
Pauline Carey

My gift to myself was a 1965 Bonneville convertible. I saw an ad in the paper saying that my friends who owned a car lot had one for sale. I immediately called Ben Hopkins, who had the ad, and asked him about it. He and his wife came over that evening and brought the car. We did all sorts of figuring, and then my husband Bob said, "We will let you know." After talking and talking about it, his decision was that we could not afford it.

After days of looking around for another car, I decided for myself that I could afford it. So I called Ben and went out and bought the car. My husband was shocked, but since I had truly always wanted both a convertible and a Bonneville, he guessed it would be okay.

I loved that car with all my heart. I enjoyed every moment of owning it. I only gave it up when we moved to Bull Shoals Lake, which had rock roads. It didn't work there. But I had many years of joy from my gift to myself.

❀ Kyky the Elephant
Margaret F. Shive

It was 1964 and I had recently arrived in Bangkok, Thailand. My husband, a pilot for Air America, was stationed in Saigon, and I had intended to join him there. However, after two visits to Saigon, one five-day visa and one fifteen-day visa, it was decided that I would set up housekeeping in Bangkok. We agreed that I was not psychologically suited to live life in a war zone. I would see him every six weeks when leave was granted.

After several weeks of settling into a compound in Bangkok and learning about areas of the city that were a short distance away, I began to realize how very much there was to learn about the people and the culture of this exotic city. And so I would do just that. At first I took short bus trips around and about the city. Later there were days spent walking the streets of the business district and market places.

Time passed and I became brave enough to venture outside the city. One day my friend Evelyn and I boarded a bus that was making a three-hour round-trip to a village close by. The old rattletrap of a vehicle was crowded with passengers: old men and women, a dozen children, two chickens, a wiry little monkey in a tiny cage, one dog, and one goat. The trip was hot and dusty. At our destination, the bus parked in the village square and most of the passengers departed, leaving Evelyn and me, a couple of locals, and a small man leading a very big, dusty, evil-smelling elephant around a water trough.

That was the first interesting experience of the day. If I could have known what was yet to come, I would not have gotten off the bus.

After looking us over carefully, the elephant's master came near and introduced himself as Pak, and in broken English, gave us a friendly welcome. After some conversation that I understood little of, I realized he had offered us a ride on the elephant. Evelyn said no. I accepted. I was introduced to Kyky, the elephant. Helped by Pak to climb the rope ladder, I got seated in a small wooden chairlike contraption on the round topside of this huge beast. Led by Pak, Kyky lumbered slowly around the village square while the wooden seat and I slipped, slid, and rocked uneasily backward, forward, and side to side. Even with this distraction, I was enjoying the adventure I knew I'd never experience again. However, Evelyn was not. With much yelling and gesturing of hands, Pak finally understood that she wanted me down on the ground with her. The elephant was commanded to stop. I gripped the arms of the little chair and fumbled with my right foot to find the first rung of the rope ladder. I missed and began to fall. It was not exactly a fall. More like a slow, everlasting slide down the rough hide of the animal, while Pak jumped up and down on the ground, madly waving his arms and yelling, "No Missy! No Missy!"

My fall knocked Pak onto his back, and I sprawled on top of him. For a second or two, we lay in this position on the hard, dusty ground, both embarrassed but neither hurt. So that Pak would not lose face, I immediately apologized for my stupid mishap. I assured him over and over that he could have done no differently. Then I rose groggily to my feet and staggered gratefully toward Evelyn and the haven of the bus.

I have a foot-high bronze-colored replica of an elephant that stands on a small oriental chest in my living room. His name is Kyky.

❀ Outward Bound
Jeanie Forsyth

Outward Bound was a test of body and spirit and held some of the high points and low points of my life.

It was May 1974; I was forty-seven. Spring term at UT [the University of Texas] was nearing the end, and I was planning a trip to New York to see my daughter Nancy. But she had a new love—not the best time for Mom's visit. My friend Summer suggested an alternative, Outward Bound. She'd done it the previous year and had only good things to say about the experience. It began in three weeks, but maybe there would be a space for me. I got on the waiting list, and started jogging every morning. The call came. I was *in*.

Texas Outward Bound: Big Bend in June. Temperatures over a hundred every day. Most of the participants were in their late teens. I was in the "geriatric patrol," and the oldest by fifteen years in that patrol. All the others had been training for three months. After an endless trip out of Alpine in the bed of a pickup truck, we gathered in a field in late afternoon to pick up our gear. There were only three of us women—Brooke, Joanne, and me—in my patrol and five men, inexperienced outdoors people all, except for our patrol leader, Greg. Joanne from Massachusetts, in Texas for the first time, and I, got the giggles when we first put on our packs, not believing we'd really be carrying that much weight (forty pounds), and naively expecting that we would be camping there for the night. The ordeal— er . . . um—the challenge began.

We hiked out that first evening, making camp just before dark. Three and a half weeks in the rugged outdoors were ahead. We bushwhacked across the desert and climbed and slid and fell through rock canyons; I fell down a great many times and always, it seemed, on my poor knees. Usually, I was bringing up the rear of the line. The others would stop to rest and as soon as I caught up, off they went again—no rest for me. We learned rock climbing, belaying, rappelling. Rappelling was easy and fun, climbing that rock face a triumph, and always there was more. Rafting down the Rio Grande, the rapids, the calm waters—I thought that would give my body ease. Wrong. Paddling was hard work, it was hot, and I got sunburned. One night, making camp after dark, my gear was wet and I put it down in an ant bed, a real low point. Our last three days we did our solos in the Chisos Mountains and the following morning hiked down to base camp, now a group of seasoned adventurers.

Sometimes it had seemed those days would never end. But I stuck with it, one of the hardest and most rewarding things I've ever done. The best dividend has been a long-term friendship with my fellow sufferer Joanne, and also, I suppose, simply having met the challenge of that summer in the wilds of Texas.

✿ The Happiest Day of My Life
Erma Hiltpold

The happiest day of my life takes me back all of thirty-five years. At the time I had just completed a two-year correspondence course in journalism from Oklahoma University. For some unknown reason, or maybe not so unknown, I had always wanted to write. In school, if I were encouraged by a good grade on themes or in compositions, I never failed to show my mother. Although she normally was noncommittal, I took her silence to mean that she approved.

It goes without saying that at this time I had never seen a rejection slip, much less received one. However, I braved the bugaboo editor of a national magazine with a timid submission. The rejection came back promptly. Every word seemed thoughtfully kind and almost apologetic, but there was no way I could interpret a favorable response. I vowed this would be my secret. No one, but no one, would know of my failure. Thus, I retired to my lonely corner to lick my wounds along with all the other thousands of writers out there.

I would, however, survive and while recovering, it seemed only smart and worthwhile to read as many trade journals available on the writers' market. I was impressed with them all. But the outstanding one, in my opinion, was *The Writer*, with its bimonthly poetry workshop conducted by Maxine Kumin, a nationally known poet and writer. With her in mind, I slowly wrote a poem for her to critique for me, if I could be so fortunate.

It was a long wait for the next issue of *The Writer*, which I had subscribed to earlier. Immediately I turned to the workshop section. In bold print there was my poem, "Television." I was astonished. Thankful that no one was with me, I sang, I danced, and I hugged myself, repeating, "I didn't think I could do it! I didn't think it possible!" The tears began to flow and I dried my eyes to read her long column of critique, knowing that everyone was not so lucky as I. I reveled in her words of praise, which overshadowed the critical remarks I certainly could not differ with. After all, who could contest a voice of authority so compelling, or one beautiful moment to always be remembered?

I have published several poems since and one small article (the only one, in fact, I was ever paid for). None has brought me the joy and satisfaction of the first.

✽ The Day My Daughter Walked
Mary Holder

One of the happiest times of my life was when we brought our baby girl home from the hospital. She still could not walk—she had been in the hospital for about three months with polio. We gave her exercise every day and worked with her. One day my mother-in-law came to visit, and we decided to take Diane out of the bed and see if she could walk at all. She had a hard time getting started but finally made it across the room. She started laughing so hard, just like she understood what had happened. While she was laughing so hard, her grandmother and I were crying, but they were tears of joy. Months of prayers had finally been answered.

❀ I Felt like a Queen
Lorene B. Laird

One of my happy memories centers around the senior year of my college life. During a senior class meeting, our duty was to choose a representative as senior candidate for Ranger Queen. When my name was placed in nomination, I got this feeling of apprehension, but when I was selected to represent the seniors, I was ecstatic.

The next several days were spent getting together a costume to wear in the parade. I had a lovely pink evening gown and one of my friends wanted me to wear her fur jacket. I really thought I looked rather grand, and felt like a queen riding on the float in the parade! This was a great culminating moment of my college life.

Of course, the freshman representative got to be the Ranger Queen, since there were many more freshmen than seniors in school. But just being a part of this celebration was a memorable time for me, and one I shall always treasure.

❀ A Summer with Granny Rylee
Pat Williamson

I remember a summer with Granny Rylee, my maternal grandmother. I was about ten years old and Granny, my little brother Mike, and I boarded a train to go from where we lived in Odessa, Texas, to Granny's in Cisco.

Granny would let us do almost anything we wanted. We made "snuff" out of cocoa and sugar. We played her old Victrola that my cousin Sonny had given her when he went off to

World War II. He gave her all of his old records of Russ Columbo, Bing Crosby, Glenn Miller, and other popular bands of the time, and we played them over and over. Granny loved going to the movies, so we'd walk to town and see the Saturday matinee with the serials, previews, Movietone News, and then the movie. Any character Granny didn't like was either an "old hussy" or a "scalawag." If there was a man in the movie that Granny *really* didn't like, he was "not worth a hill of beans" or a "no-count."

Granny's house was always clean, but I don't remember her spending that much time on housework when Mike and I were there that summer. She spent most of her time with us. Granny was the one who taught me to play solitaire and work the crossword puzzle in the newspaper.

Many times, Mike and I would get into Granny's chifforobe to get old hats or other clothes Aunt Opal (one of Mother's older sisters who was a twin to Aunt Jewel) had given her and act out the movies we saw. Granny was a good actress herself, very good at "make-believe," and encouraged us to do this and would join in when we wanted her to. Mostly, she was our audience.

Jackie Douglas and her family lived next door, and they had a huge old oak tree in their yard, which was wonderful for climbing. When we played "Tarzan," Jackie would be Jane, Mike would be Boy, and I always had to be Tarzan, because I was the biggest. I loved climbing that tree. Back home in Odessa, we didn't have trees big enough to climb, so if I wanted to get up high, I'd have to go to the neighbor's windmill and climb it. (Mother said I was a born climber. When I was really little, I used to climb up on the cabinets, so that I could then climb up on the refrigerator to sit up there.)

Sometimes Granny, Mike, and I would play cards and drink "wine" made out of Kool-Aid, served out of the wine decanter and matching glasses given to Granny by Uncle Earl, Mother's youngest brother. We felt very special and grown-up when given that treat.

At night, we would snuggle up to Granny and she would

tell us stories. This was one of our favorite things, as Granny was the best storyteller in the world, and we could hardly wait for bedtime.

We always spent a lot of time with Granny because my mother was very close to her and wanted us to be close to her too. But there was something really magical about that summer of 1947.

CHAPTER EIGHT

Witness

Ordinary Lives, Extraordinary Events

The OWL Circle memoirists have lived through a succession of historically momentous events and accelerating social change. In every decade of their adulthood, American women and men now over sixty have been witness to war, and those in their nineties can still recall the Great War, the war to end all war. They have seen the waxing and waning of Cold War consciousness, the Nuclear Age, man on the moon, global politics, the Internet —sweeping cultural changes that, by century's end, had transformed many of the assumptions and expectations they had spent a lifetime learning.

In human terms, the cumulative effect of these changes remains ambiguous, and the OWL Circle women's response to them is ambivalent. The world has grown larger, and women are free to travel, but home is where the heart is. Feminism has expanded women's power and professional prestige, but the career culture is still largely a man's world. Civil rights activism has forged a more integrated society, but one that still fosters hate crime.

When they write about the historical events that have shaped their lives, women over sixty best remember their country's wars, and how war and its aftermath shaped their lives. Sometimes they remember the sound of German boots marching through the streets and Hitler's speeches on the radio, while they and their families huddled in fear. Sometimes they recall a special day, such as Pearl Harbor Day, or the day Franklin Roosevelt or John Kennedy or Martin Luther King died, but they always remember the day in terms of their lives and the lives of their families: where they were, what they were doing, how they felt. For them, history is not just the large event, but the event clothed in human significance.

We are all witnesses to history. But these women, who have lived for sixty, seventy, eighty, even ninety years and more, have seen an entire century unfold, a century of incredible violence and equally incredible accomplishment. Their stories help us to gain perspective on our own experience; their testimony enables us to see the extraordinary past in terms of ordinary human lives.

Remembering War
Mathilda Mimun

(Mathilda Mimun, a non-native speaker of English, asked that her writing appear unedited.)

It was 1939, the World War Two bring bad memory. I remember when the Germans pass by in the street in group and they make that noise when they march it just scare you. Often we hear the siren and we all have to go down. We lived in the second floor so we go to the first floor at a neighbor. I remember how hard it was for my poor father who was blind and we all set together and pray. We hear planes going over us, and we hope they'll go away. We hear bombs falling near us, it's so scary. When we hear the second siren we all go out and we look what building came down. At that time I was twelve years old, and was living in Tunisia, I was going to school before it start it but then there was no more school.

The moment I heard the news I was with my mother shopping. I can see my mother worry and was asking her, what happen, and she told me it's going to be a war. At that time I didn't know what to think or what going to happen, but I was scared. I knew it wasn't good news. During the war we have to wait in line for everything; bread, meat, groceries, and everything was rationed. We didn't have a washing machine or electric stove. My mother cooked with charcoal and kerosene and we have to wait in line for that, too. To buy a piece of meat we get up at three in the morning to stay in line. We were a family of seven so at each meal my mother divided everything by seven and if we want more, it's too bad.

Holocaust Survivor
Sarah Lichtman

It was 1939. The atmosphere in Poland was very bad. The anti-Semitism was everywhere, but the most scary thing was to listen to the radio and hear Hitler's speeches. We were all hoping that the war would not come, but we were very wrong. Poland was occupied in three days. It was October 1939, a beautiful sunny day. All of Sunday we heard terrible noises, as the Germans were already bombing the city. I was terrified as I went home. I was very afraid of bombing, and the whole family decided to go to my grandmother's home, hoping that this would be safe. We were very wrong; the bombing was even worse. So we left my grandfather's house and decided to go home.

When I was a young girl, I belonged to an organization called Haszomer Haruir. This was a Zionist group. We wanted to go to Israel and live in a kibbutz, a collective. Before the war we used to get together to dance the hora and sing Hebrew songs. We also had a leader who conducted lectures twice a week, and we used to learn a lot. We wanted to live in Israel and help to build the country. Two from the organization were able to get certificates and go to Israel (you had to have a certificate from the English who ruled at this time in Israel). The rest of my friends died in a concentration camp in Treblinka or Auschwitz and other camps. I am the lucky one who survived.

✤ "Where Is Pearl Harbor?"
Lavern Crawford

I was seventeen years old, living at home and taking postgraduate courses in sciences and chemistry. I was just waiting to fulfill the age requirement of eighteen to enter nursing school at Northwest Texas State in Amarillo, Texas, in September 1942. I was getting ready to leave home for the first time, and trying to arrange a wardrobe that included white hose and shoes, with extra shoelaces and white shoe polish. I had my own radio and suitcase. I was also busy getting my physical and dental exams and inoculations.

On Sunday evening my sister and I attended a picture show

called *Ship-Ahoy,* a light musical with lots of sailors. When we got home we heard the news, and the first thought I had was "Where is Pearl Harbor?" Then, "How dare the Japs!" My dad was concerned that we would be pulled into another World War.

By March of 1942, a special Emergency Class was formed to meet the demand for more nurses, and I was accepted along with twelve others. For such a small class, we became a close group, strong enough to stand up to the larger class of thirty-five. We passed the State Board, received our diplomas, and did essential nursing.

 ## December 7, 1941
Jean Leonard

On December 6, 1941, I turned sixteen years old. This was such a special time in our circle of girlfriends. Usually there was a party to go to. My parents told me we were celebrating by going to Radio City Music Hall. Oh, well, no party for me! So we went out to a special show, had dinner, and came home. I was so weary but happy to be with Momma and Poppa. "It was better than a party," I said to myself.

We went to the elevator in our apartment building, but Momma said she'd forgotten her key. So she rang the bell at the door. It was opened by my big brother and sister with a greeting of "Surprise! Surprise!" The lights went on, and there were all my girlfriends and boyfriends from our crowd. What a fun evening we had. My big brother and sister planned this whole event for me.

The next morning I expected calls from friends telling me what a great time they had. No calls! I told Momma that perhaps they really didn't enjoy the party. My brother, a policeman, walked in at 9 A.M. after a midnight shift. His face was downcast. He asked, "Did you hear on the radio that Pearl Harbor was bombed by the Japanese?"

So that's the memory I have of my sweet sixteenth birthday and Pearl Harbor.

❀ How Would I Measure Up under Fire?
Eileen C. Titus

I grew up in England and lived in a small town twenty miles from London. The reality of World War II really began for me with the first large air raid on London, in September 1940. It was a beautiful, sunny, late summer day, too pretty for such a dire event.

I was working as a telephone operator, and knew that something unusual was happening by the great volume of telephone calls, so many that my arms ached from handling the cords. Returning home for tea, my dad said, "Something is going on, planes overhead all afternoon." At 6 P.M. we listened to the news on the radio. There had been a huge raid on London, and the docks were burning. We walked to where we could see to the south, where the fires were reflected in the sky.

Dark thoughts came to me. How many people had died that day, how many more raids would there be? Was this the beginning of the threatened German invasion?

How would I measure up under fire?

❀ Rommel's Hannibal Connection
Janine M. Koch

As a child of eight or nine, growing up in Hannibal, Missouri, I felt very content with my life and family. All of our activities centered around the family. An important part of our day was dinnertime, when we were all together.

One night at dinner, my dad announced that he had heard that some of Rommel's troops were coming to Hannibal to be housed at Clemens Field until the end of the war. I didn't have a clue who Rommel was but felt fairly certain that he was someone pretty important. I wondered if the Germans would try to come to Hannibal to free them. My dad reassured me that everything would be fine. He told me that these men were just like our boys who were fighting overseas. They were someone's relatives, and their families worried about them, like we worried about our troops. My brothers thought the whole idea was exciting.

When the troop train came to town, there were a lot of townspeople who went to see what was happening. In a very orderly fashion, the troops were marched from the depot to Clemens Field, which was only a few blocks. The soldiers walked with their hands fastened behind their heads, and there were no problems.

Clemens Field was at that time the largest enclosure of its kind in the world. It had been built by the WPA during the Depression, and the walls were about two feet thick and eight or ten feet tall. I'm not sure just why it was built, but the city uses it now to house about four ball fields. This was during the fall of the year, which is a beautiful time in the Midwest. The nights would be cool and the days pleasantly warm. The soldiers lived in tents. They worked at the shoe factory and were marched with their hands behind their heads with armed guards to and from the factory.

Having Rommel's troops in Hannibal made me more aware of the war than a young girl needed to be. I did not have a lot of fear about the prisoners who were there, as they seemed to be guarded very well. A fear that I had was that the Japanese soldiers might come across the bridge in tanks and torture people. I don't think I ever told anyone how scared I was about that issue. The Mark Twain bridge was a beautiful new bridge connecting Missouri to Illinois, but the thought of Japanese tanks gave it a whole new perspective in my young eyes.

During the war, the family listened to the radio regularly, especially to President Roosevelt's fireside chats. We also had to prepare for air raid drills, which were held on a regular basis, always at night, and always unannounced. This meant that everyone had to go inside their homes and pull the shades down and turn off all lights so that enemy planes could not see any light from the air. This was very scary. My dad was an air raid warden. He had to go out and patrol the neighborhood to see that everyone was in compliance.

The war also brought about many changes in regular family life. Everything was in short supply. We had ration stamps for everything. Since we did not have a car, our family could trade gasoline stamps for stamps for meat with someone who needed extra gasoline stamps. It was the beginning of the recycling period. Everything was saved for the war effort. I remember one Fourth of July, my brother and I wanted to decorate his bike for a parade. We found gum wrappers and peeled the tin foil off the paper and put it on the spokes. It looked great!

As an adult, just a few years ago, I went to the library to research the Rommel stories and was surprised to see that the newspaper gave it very little coverage. I guess things just look bigger to a child.

 Not a Dry Eye in the House
Patricia J. Click

As the war's first year wore into what became known as "the duration," I was teaching in my hometown, courtesy of an emergency certificate. I had only two years of college, but with all the able-bodied men gone to the services, I was allowed to teach.

My friend Rena Beth, who taught sixth grade, was a musician, so we got together and planned a bond-selling program. I wrote the program—long on patriotic songs and the Gettysburg Address, and so forth. Not being musical at all, I had the chutzpah to direct the chorus, while Rena Beth played the piano. We discovered two unusual voices, and arranged for them to sing solos. One was a scamp in my seventh-grade room whose voice had changed, and who had an almost grown-up baritone. He sang a medley of service songs attired in a motley World War I uniform. He was a sensation! The other soloist was a precocious five-year-old girl with blond ringlets and an astounding voice. When she finished the program with "God Bless America," there wasn't a dry eye in the house.

We sold lots of war bonds!

❀ When the Americans Came
Jean Wyllys

As children, Dorothy and I used to spend a lot of time on our bicycles, riding around Cornwall. It was safe in those days. We lived in a rural area, and it wasn't considered dangerous for two young girls to ride alone around the countryside. It was also safe as far as the war was concerned, and children were evacuated to our town from London.

I can't remember how we became aware that there were Americans in our area. But one day, topping a rise on our bicycles, we saw a huge camp spread out below us, where previously there had been just heather. The American invasion had begun.

We were too young to know what was really going on. Obviously, we knew there was a war in progress, but we didn't know that America had become involved. However, Americans and their very large vehicles began to appear in our small town. I was downtown one day when an American truck (we called them lorries, of course) bashed into a building and knocked a piece off the corner of it. I heard the driver say, "We'll widen their streets for them."

As a young and innocent girl, I remember the Americans in the blackout. (For someone who has never experienced a blackout, it might be difficult to imagine living in a town where after sunset there was no light at all, anywhere—except, of course, from the moon, if there was one.) The only social thing I did as a teenager was to attend girls' club at my church, and I had to walk home afterward in the blackout. I'd approach a crossroads and I'd become aware of a circle of glowing cigarette ends ahead of me in the dark. I'd hear a voice say, "I'll take this one," and then, "Hello, darling, can I walk you home?"

"No, thank you," I'd say in my prissy accent, my face flaming in the concealing darkness, and I'd quicken my steps to get away. Only many years later did I come to understand a bit about what those very young American men, miles from home and in a strange and hostile environment, might have been feeling.

During the war, the beaches were all mined and fenced off with barbed wire against a possible invasion. There was a large American camp in the cliffs near a favorite beach of ours. What we called the seal cave, where the seals came every year to have their pups, was a huge cave, not readily accessible to humans, but apparently just right for American grenade practice. After the grenade practice, the seals never came back.

In recalling these very small incidents in a very large war, I feel again the resentment we felt then against the Americans. They had invaded our safe and quiet world with their brash loudness, their sophisticated ways, their nylons, and their chocolate (and subsequently their babies), and nothing, it seemed, would ever be the same. Now, when I return to England as an American, I am resentful of the prejudice against Americans, which still seems to pervade the country. In writing this memoir, I think I understand the roots of that prejudice. What I don't understand is why it has gone on so long.

❀ The Day Roosevelt Died
Bobbye Jo Barker

It was April 1945. World War II would end the following August. I was sixteen years old and living in Dallas with my family.

I was a senior in high school, self-absorbed like most teenagers. That day I was riding the bus home from school, noticing what a warm and sunny day it was. Someone, the driver I think, asked the few passengers on the bus if they had heard that the President had died. We were all shocked and speechless. I could not believe what I had just heard, and thought it must be a mistake. Franklin Roosevelt had been President as long as I could remember. The bus stopped to let a man off. As he stepped down the stairs he yelled over his shoulder, "I'm glad he's gone."

I got off at the next stop and ran the one long block to our house. My mother was sitting by the radio, crying, and I knew it was true. The President was dead. As other members of my family arrived home from work, they joined us by the radio to hear the reports from Washington and Warm Springs, where the President was when he died. Everyone, even my father, cried. We all wondered what would happen to us, to our country. We could not imagine life without this man to lead us, especially with the war still being fought. Like many others across the country, we were devastated.

The nation went into mourning. I can remember Arthur Godfrey, the radio commentator, crying as he described the funeral procession, with the riderless horse being led down Pennsylvania Avenue in Washington, D.C. The radio stations canceled their regular programs and in their place gave any news pertaining to the President's death, and filled the rest of their airtime with appropriate music. I was at a friend's house and her mother angrily turned off the radio saying, "I can't stand that funeral dirge any longer."

Roosevelt was a man you loved or hated. There didn't seem to be a middle ground. No one was indifferent toward him, living or dead. The nation did survive. Harry Truman, a man we knew little about, became President, and the war continued. A lasting memory of those days was a picture of President Roosevelt's constant companion, a small Scottish terrier named Fala, standing alone in front of the family home in Hyde Park, New York, where his master had just been buried.

⚜ An Army Wife in Postwar Germany
Faye B. Kelly

(Excerpted from a longer memoir)

After the war in Europe was over, Bruce transferred to the military government in Germany to keep (he thought) from going to the Pacific to fight Japan. He declared adamantly that he was no hero, even though he had won a Silver Star and a Purple Heart.

In July of 1946 he was allowed to come home from TDY (temporary duty). He had come home with military orders for the children and me to accompany him back to Germany. However, the military command in the U.S. would not recognize orders issued in the ETO (European Theater of Operations). That meant that the children and I had to make the trip alone. It took some time for me to get all the arrangements made to start on our great adventure. In fact, I feel I might have been still sitting there waiting for the Army to do something if I had not enlisted the aid of my senator from Florida, Claude Pepper. In complete disgust with the Army, I took off for a weekend at the beach. On my return home, my front porch was littered with telegrams with instructions for me to be on my way to Fort Hamilton, New York. As I remember, this was early fall.

Another woman from Gainesville and her two children went on the same train with us to the staging area in Brooklyn. Everywhere I looked in the camp were dependents' quarters, dependents' mess, dependents' infirmary. After three and a half years on my own, holding down a teaching job and caring for two children, I certainly did not feel dependent on anybody. After about a week in Brooklyn we were all herded (that is the only word that fits) onto a converted troop ship, where we were quartered on the ship according to our husbands' rank. That meant that the wives and children of majors and colonels were bedded in a large compartment, with at least twenty people in double-decker bunks. I facetiously remarked that the only difference between us and sardines was that they did not bathe us in oil first. My children by this time were old enough that they both wanted the upper berth. One of the other occupants of our compartment was a Mrs. Thompson, accompanied by her eighteen-year-old daughter, whom she had taken out of college to make the trip to Germany. When I inquired about the advisability of taking the girl out of college, the mother replied that she hoped her daughter would meet some nice young officer and marry him. I am pleased to report that she met and married John Eisenhower. Nice work for Mama.

On the voyage, the commander gathered all the women in the so-called ballroom, where he lectured on how we should conduct ourselves in Germany. The first sentence of his lecture was, "Remember you are going into an occupied country, and a good German is a dead German." My one close contact in the U.S. with a German was with an uncle by marriage who looked just like everybody else to me, but who was perhaps more industrious than many other members of my family.

After almost a week on the Atlantic we landed at Bremerhaven. From there we went by train to Frankfurt, where we were met by my husband and transported to Wiesbaden, where we were domiciled at *acht-und-zwanzig* Rheinblich Strasse. But in order to get a glimpse of the Rhine, we had to go up to the third floor, get out on the balcony, and lean far out. Our house was in a compound surrounded by a fence and guarded by Polish soldiers. When we got well acquainted with some Germans, there was a joke going around that said the Americans thought the guards were to protect them, but actually the guards were to protect the Germans from the Americans.

The task of housekeeping and procuring food became a time-consuming chore. Ostensibly the Army had provided for all our needs, but many gaps had to be filled in. I had a housekeeper-cook, but when she came the morning after we had arrived and greeted me with "Good morning, Mrs. Kelly," she had used her complete vocabulary of English. Just communicating with Suze was a full-time job until I had mastered enough *Kuchen Deutsch* to run the house. Since this was the first time in my life I had full-time servants, I had imagined that my stay in Germany would be uninterrupted bliss. Little did I anticipate the daily quarrels I would have to settle between Suze and Fritz, the gardener who spoke with a thick Prussian dialect. In fact, I had to learn two different languages, some of which had to be cleaned up by Frau von Haehling, my husband's secretary, before I could go out in polite society.

One ever-present, almost insurmountable task was getting food into the house to feed my family properly. My one and only legal source for food was the military commissary, where for three months after I had arrived in Wiesbaden, the only vegetable was canned peas. To this day I can barely face peas. As a result of the paucity of fruits and vegetables, the entire family suffered from constant sore throats. A young Army doctor told us our problem was caused by a lack of Vitamin C and gave us some pills. Then and there, I determined that, fraternization or no fraternization, I was going to find fresh vegetables. The first thing we did was to plant all the flowerbeds around the house with lettuce, mustard, and turnip seeds. While we waited for these seeds to produce, I made contact with a man who was able to procure for me some root vegetables: carrots, rutabagas, potatoes, and cabbage. The farmer preserved these vegetables in mounds of earth that he opened periodically. When most of the German people were suffering, this farmer said all he needed was ear rings for his pigs.

Before I went to Germany I had fancied myself as a thrifty housewife, but with the German people suffering in a war-torn country with all the necessities of life in short supply, I saw first-hand what real thrift could be. Suze told me she fed her dog cooked *Kartoffel Schalen* (potato peelings). Frau von Haehling would use a tea bag several times. A young Catholic priest we met loved tea but could not get any, so he became one of my clients. Suze, my housekeeper, could get black bread (a dark whole-wheat bread) and all I could get was white bread, so we exchanged. Suze absolutely could not understand why we liked dark bread. We also gathered into our circle of recipients a niece of my German uncle. She was a student at the University of Frankfurt and could ride the bus to Wiesbaden. When she came

WITH COURAGE AND COMMON SENSE

to see us we would load her up with food. I shall never forget her delight when my husband killed a hare and gave it to her, still in its skin. That provided her with several pounds of good meat. Even I learned to make *Hasen Rücken* and *Hasen Pfeffer*, which my family ate with gusto. Spam was the main meat we got from the commissary, except for canned salmon. I still cannot stand Spam. Nor did I ever get used to the powdered eggs or powdered milk. We got fresh milk shipped in from Holland for the children, but not for the adults.

One attempt on the part of the military government to alleviate the critical situation among the German people and perhaps cut down on the black market trade was to establish a barter mart in Frankfurt where the Germans could bring items to sell to the Americans. We bought some crystal wine glasses, some of which made it back to the U.S. As long as my husband was alive, we always had a drink of German wine from our German glasses on our wedding anniversary. I have some very fond memories of Germany and of some German people.

Our social life was restricted by military protocol except for events at the officers' club, where I learned to appreciate good German beer and wine, especially white wine and the best brandy in Europe, *Asbach Uralt*. I still try to find a bottle at Christmas time as "medicine" (called by the Germans, *Grippen Torter:* flu killer). We did break the nonfraternization policy and entertained a professor from the University of Frankfurt and his wife. He introduced himself as Herr Doctor Null von de Nama and his wife as Frau Doctor von de Nama. They were a charming couple. I remember little about them except that when my husband passed the biscuits at dinner, the professor took one, held it up, looked at it, and said, "Ah biscuit, *Gone with the Wind*." It seems that he had read about biscuits in the book but had never seen or eaten one.

One other occasion with a German, on an informal basis, involved a sick dog. My husband had purchased two German setters, which he had hoped to bring back to America. However, both contracted a virulent type of distemper that had begun in Spain and was working its way throughout Europe. Naturally we called a veterinarian, who managed to call on his "patients" right at breakfast time. Of course we invited him to have breakfast with us. The remarkable thing about this experience was that the two men, recently enemies, could sit at the table together and discuss objectively the battles of the war they had both been in. While I sat silently and listened to them, I realized that ordinary Germans had no more to do with starting the war than ordinary Americans had.

Another facet of life in postwar Germany that affected everybody was the economy. Inflation was rampant, and cigarettes became the only viable medium of exchange. Cigarettes were available to Americans at the Post Exchange, though rationed one carton for each person per week. Since neither of us smoked, we had two cartons a week for other purposes. Each week I gave Suze one package of cigarettes, which would purchase more than her entire salary for the week from the military government. Whenever we went out to eat at any event staged by Americans, we always left as a tip a couple of cigarettes by our plate instead of military script. One incident I remember vividly happened on the street in front of the commissary. An American soldier threw a half-smoked cigarette onto the street almost directly at my feet, where I stood waiting for the bus. A dignified German man in *Lederhosen* and a Tyrolean hat, striding along with his walking cane with a spike on the end, thought he would spear the butt. But before he could, a German woman almost knocked me off my feet as she swooped down and snagged the cigarette. She looked up triumphantly at the man and said, *"Mein Mann raucht auch"* (My husband smokes also). Incidents such as this brought home to me the pervasive influence of war on every facet of human life. . . .

❀ An Ordinary Day: An Extraordinary Event
Wanda Heath

I was living in Hollidaysburg, Pennsylvania, at the time of the Kennedy assassination. I was a young mother with two very young children—Brad was twenty-one months old and Glenn was only three months. My next-door neighbor, Rae, also had a son who was three months old, and she had come over for coffee and to share motherly tips while both our husbands were at work and her four older children were in school. The TV was on in the background as we visited.

When I picked Glenn up, I noticed his diaper was wet, so I walked up a few steps to the nursery, followed by both Rae and Brad. Suddenly the TV broke the news, and Rae and I stared at each other in disbelief. I said to her, "Do you realize that this day will probably be the most significant date in our lifetimes, and when we think about what we were doing when we heard about it, it will be changing diapers."

I guess that's how it was for many of us. We were doing ordinary things in our ordinary lives when something extraordinary shocked us into realizing how fortunate we were to have our families safe in a world where it could all disappear so easily.

Terror: The Day MLK Died
Louise Kent

In the late sixties, I was working in downtown Washington, D.C., at the Department of Commerce, which was located about two blocks from the White House and in the midst of the shopping district—lots of shops, department stores, restaurants, and businesses. If you've ever lived in Washington, D.C., you are aware that the various government departments employ thousands and thousands of people who live in the suburbs, as do a great majority of the employees of the various businesses. At that time the majority of the residents of Washington were black.

The announcement had come on the radio that Dr. Martin Luther King, Jr., had been shot and killed. In the late morning the discontent started with small groups of black people rioting to protest Dr. King's murder. At first, it was a neighborhood occurrence, but as the day progressed, so did the number of people involved. Businesses were closing and sending their employees home; the government closed. Thousands of people were trying to leave Washington at the same time. One of my coworkers insisted that I come in her car with her boyfriend rather than go on the bus, which was my usual mode of transportation to Maryland where I lived. I gratefully accepted and called my children to let them know I was on my way home, but it would probably take a while and there would be no way I could contact them while en route—no cell phones in those days!

The three of us got in the car and started our long terrifying ride home. Just picture this: thousands of people trying to leave Washington at the same time. No matter which street we were on, it was bumper-to-bumper traffic and all around us the blacks were rioting—overturning cars, knocking down people who were in the way, breaking store windows, and stealing the goods from the shops and stores. And the noise! A constant yelling and screaming. As we inched along, even the sound of a low-hanging tree branch scraping cross the top of the car was horrifying!

After what seemed an eternity, we made it out of the city. The traffic was still heavy, but it was moving. We had to stop for gas, and we turned and looked back at the city. What a shock! Fires had been started at various places, and since it was dark now, we could see the flames shooting into the night. That sight filled me with such great sorrow.

On a normal day my bus ride from work would take about thirty-five to forty-five minutes. This car ride from hell had taken over five hours. I can testify that to be terrified for that length of time is emotionally draining. By the time I arrived home I was numb.

To me, the worst thing was that all of this mayhem—the killings, the maiming of people, the destroying of property and goods, the fires—was done as a protest against the death of Dr. King, a man who had spent his life preaching goodness, love, unity, and the coming together of all races. How sad.

When the Russians Invaded Czechoslovakia
Dolores R. Muhich

(Excerpted from a longer memoir)

In the summer of 1968, I assisted Dr. Kupcek, head of the Russian Department at Southern Illinois University at Carbondale, on a ten-week foreign language study tour to the then USSR . . .

When we deplaned in Moscow, it was raining. It rained for our entire stay there, not a hard rain, just a drizzle. Lenin's body lay in state in Red Square. We stood in a line that stretched for several blocks before entering the Mausoleum, an underground, refrigerated chamber where cameras were not allowed. St. Basil's Cathedral was under renovation. Scaffolding surrounded the building, and its various bright colors were all faded. The artwork inside was also under renovation.

From Moscow we flew to Sochi, which was a pleasant and welcome change. Here it was warm and sunny and the sandy beaches stretched for miles. We sunbathed, swam in the Black Sea, and toured a Young Pioneers Camp (similar to our Scouts) in the Caucasus Mountains. The young people put on a great show for us.

Our final exam took place on a boat ride leaving Sochi on our way to Romania. Here, we had to board a train on our way to Czechoslovakia. The train kept moving and would not stop for us. While the train was moving slowly, we had to run after it with our baggage and jump aboard. There was no seating for us. That leg of our journey was the low point of our trip. . . .

From Prague, we went to Comenius University in Bratislava. While we were housed in the dormitories, an invasion by the Russian tanks took place during the night. I felt a cold coming on, so I took a Contact capsule before going to bed that evening and slept through the whole invasion. Apparently, the tanks fired, because we could see the bullet holes in some of the buildings. Tanks lined the streets when I awoke.

There was only one bridge over the Danube for entry and exit. It was patrolled by Russian guards. Austria was about five miles away. All transportation was at a standstill. People were instructed by radio broadcasts not to report to work. Our only possibility of getting to Austria, other than walking, was from a bus driver who was supposed to return later that day from Yugoslavia. Dr. Kupcek informed all the students to pack their belongings and to be ready to leave on a moment's notice. In the meantime, we tried to dispose of our *korunas*. There wasn't much to buy. Bratislava is primarily agricultural—a bread basket—and important to Russia for that purpose. I bought a large piece of cheese and secured a piece of rope for a backpack, just in case we would end up hiking the five miles to Austria.

After about two hours, the bus driver returned and agreed to take us to Austria if we left immediately. There were a few other tourists who were to board the bus with us. We put our *korunas* in a large paper bag, and the bus driver agreed to that amount. When the head count was taken, two students, Marianne and Phil, were missing. The bus driver gave us five more minutes. The two students were not found. Dr. Kupcek gave the order to leave. The male students put Phil's baggage on the bus. I left Marianne's luggage in the dorm room.

Our visas were all checked by the Russian guards before they allowed us to drive across the bridge . . . The next day, Dr. Kupcek checked with the American Embassy, and we proceeded to the accommodations previously made for us in Vienna. As we found out later, Marianne and Phil were having a romantic rendezvous. The next morning when they proceeded to leave Comenius University, Marianne was permitted to cross the bridge because she had her visa. Phil had packed his in his luggage, which his buddies put on the bus, so he was not permitted to leave. Marianne took a cab to the American Embassy, made contact with our group, secured Phil's visa, and returned to Bratislava.

While we were experiencing all the events at Comenius University, Shirley Temple Black was on a diplomatic mission in Prague . . .

Four Joyful Days
Agatha Barbay

On a very sad day, July 20, 1966, I was horrified to learn that my husband's aircraft had been shot down over North Vietnam. He and our family were to endure nearly seven years until his return after the Peace Agreement ending the Vietnam War in January 1973.

I had no indication whether Larry was alive or dead for nearly four years. Then came my first most joyful day. I was living in Baton Rouge, Louisiana (our birth place), with our four children. That morning I received a phone call from the wife of another POW from Baton Rouge. She related to me a letter she had received from her husband, in which there was a phrase that she did not understand. She read the phrase, and it contained a nickname which was not her husband's. Upon hearing the phrase, my heart was filled with joy because I knew it was Larry's nickname in high school. You see, her husband and my husband went to the same high school and played football together. That was the first indication I had that Larry was alive. I cannot even describe the wonderful feelings for my family and me. They were a combination of prayerful thanksgiving, joy, and relief.

The second most joyful day was nearly three years later, when news came that the war in Vietnam had ended and that the POWs were to be released. Again. it gave me additional faith that I would see my husband.

The third most joyful day, March 4, 1973, came when my husband called me on the telephone from Clark Air Base in the Philippine Islands. What a joy! We had four days to talk on the telephone, and then the fourth and most joyful day of all was March 8, 1973, when I held my husband in my arms. All this is proof positive that miracles still do happen.

CHAPTER NINE

Legacies
"I Wish You Could Have Known My Grandma"

Alex Haley has written, "Every time an old person dies, it is as if a library has burned down." The memoirists of the OWL Circle Project understand that very well. Everything they write is an effort to leave something behind: memories of people long dead; bits and pieces of family history; an heirloom keepsake, carefully documented; a dream; a philosophy; some words of hard-earned wisdom and insight. They know that they are the libraries of human experience. They want to leave the key in the hands of those who come after.

These memoirs are rich in legacies: books, pieces of art, a grandmother's dress, a mother's ring, a quilt, a collection of written stories. But the legacies are not just physical objects handed down in families. There is also the legacy of wisdom: a lesson learned, the view from the other side of fifty, a letter to a young person. And finally, tenderly, a writer's gentle wish that one of her grandchildren will say, someday, "I wish you could have known my grandma."

Reading their stories, hearing their words, sharing their rich treasury of memories, we can all know these women — our grandmothers, mothers, sisters, cousins, aunts. The legacy of these older women is indeed a library: of experience, knowledge, memory, wisdom. They have seen history, and lived it. It is up to us to help preserve their stories.

Family Books, Family Treasures
Helen Burnette

I like old books—actually, I like books, old or new or in between. It is no surprise that many of my treasures are books, especially books that first belonged to someone else in my family. I have some of my grandfather's books from when he was a ministerial student in seminary—one is in Greek; one is in Hebrew. The books from him are smoke-damaged because they went through the fire that destroyed the top two stories of his house. I have the bookcase, too, that they were in, still eerily marked with something like photographic negatives of books on the shelves.

I have a book of my mother's from her second grade. There is her name, carefully written: Ruth Brock. I have some of her college textbooks; some are in French. One I especially love is the French songbook. I don't know if French majors still have French songbooks as part of their studies, but at the small church-sponsored women's college she attended in the late 1920s, she did. As a child, I loved it because, although it was in French, I could still read some of the music. The notes were the same as English music! I felt that I had discovered a special key to French. The titles were easier to figure out, too, and there were some helpful decorations. And there were simply fewer baffling French words on a page of a song as contrasted with a page of text.

The oldest book I have is the most mysterious. It is a little memo book, bound in leather, with dates from the 1870s and 1860s. It is from my grandmother's family and comes from the time when they left Alabama and moved to Louisiana after the Civil War. Whose was it? I don't know. I think it was a man's book—the notes are about selling things and figuring the price per yard. It is in two pieces because the threads holding it together have come apart, but the pages and covers are in very good shape for being so old. I love to think of someone carrying it in his pocket and taking it out to jot things down. Who was he? What was his connection with me?

The Tapestry
Bobbye Jo Barker

One of my keepsakes is a tapestry that hangs on the living room wall behind our couch. It was given to my father when he was a young man, twenty-one years old, and just married. The artist who painted it was related to my father, a cousin, I think. The tapestry is fifty inches by sixty-three inches and beginning to fray in a few places, which is to be expected in something almost eighty years old.

The tapestry shows a young woman wearing a long pink gown with an overdress of light blue. Her blond hair is coiled on top of her head. She is standing in the opening of a wall, leaning slightly forward, looking far down the path in front of her, gazing at a man on horseback traveling away from where she stands. We have always assumed she was watching her lover ride away. All the colors of the tapestry—the trees, the foliage on stone wall, her dress—are soft and muted.

My parents lived in many different houses, especially during the Depression, when money was scarce and the rent had to be paid. It was pay or move, so we moved, many times. I remember that no matter how often this occurred, the tapestry was the last thing Daddy removed from the old house, and the first thing he hung at our new address. Once that happened, the place felt like home. Mother and Daddy had to give up many of their belongings through the years, but the tapestry was one possession they always kept.

After my father died, my husband Bob was the one who took over the removal and rehanging of the tapestry. This happened several times before my mother's death, the last time in my sister's house, where Mother lived the last four months of her life. My sister sold her home a year or so ago to move to smaller quarters, and decided she could not use the tapestry in her new place. I also felt I could not use it, that I had neither the space nor the decor for such a hanging. We agreed that I would bring the tapestry home and at least try to find a place for it, but with the idea of selling it if necessary. This seemed to be the sensible thing to do if none of the family could use the tapestry, but I began to feel uneasy about giving up something that has been such an important part of our family history.

A few days later, I unrolled the tapestry on our living room carpet. I was immediately struck by the way the colors in the tapestry blended with the colors in the room. To my amazement it looked beautiful. Bob hung the tapestry, measuring carefully to be sure it was centered and to satisfy my "calibrated eyeballs," as he calls them. Bob and I sat and looked at the tapestry and soon realized that it gave a warmth to the room that it had never had before. Once again, just as it had when I was a child, the tapestry had made a place feel like home.

 ## My Grandmother's Dress
Joyce A. Dehlin

Last spring, I was asked to be a docent at the quilt show in Georgetown[, Texas]. A letter arrived, giving all the specifics of time, place, and expectations. It also suggested that if I had any vintage clothing, I should wear it the day of the quilt show.

I reached back in the closet and pulled out a special dress that had belonged to my maternal grandmother, Ingrid Molin. It is a really lovely thing, of ivory voile with embroidered edges on the fabric. It is made in three pieces. The skirt has triple layers of lace and comes to about midcalf. The blouse has long, full sleeves with more lace and embroidery. The elegant ensemble is finished off with a vest that comes down just past the waist. It is in excellent condition, and I was delighted to have an occasion to wear this garment.

My pleasure in this dress goes beyond the beauty of it, as this is the story my mother told me about it.

When Mother was just a girl, she rode downtown on the streetcar with Grandma Molin, and they went to the fabric department at the Golden Rule Department Store in St. Paul.

Grandmother looked at several beautiful pieces and during the process of handling bolts of material, somehow cut her hand. Perhaps she caught it on a pin or a sharp edge of the counter. Mom did not remember just how, but it bled! And blood got on the fabric! This was quite alarming to my mother, and she remembered it vividly.

Grandmother was a frugal woman and not given to indulging herself, so Mother and I wondered—did she purchase that particular fabric because her blood got on it, or was that her selection prior to being cut? We will never know.

At any rate, Grandmother sewed this wonderful garment to wear for her fiftieth birthday in 1914. I have a portrait photograph of her wearing her own beautiful creation. It is indeed a treasure and I am so happy to have it!

I plan to give this precious, special dress to my daughter Joan. My older daughter, Mary Kaye, has the wedding dress of her paternal grandmother, so I believe that Joan would enjoy having this birthday dress of about the same vintage as the wedding dress. But logic has little to do with some of our decisions concerning items of sentimental value. What I really thought was this: Grandmother was the youngest in her family, Mother was the youngest in her family, I was the youngest in my family, and Joan is the youngest in our family. Therefore, Joan should have the dress.

My Mother's Ring
Mathilda Mimun

(Mathilda Mimun, a non-native speaker of English, asked that her writing appear unedited.)

My keepsake is the ring I'm wearing on my finger. My mother gave it to me when I was leaving for America. It was a very hard time for my mother, she knew I was going very far away and didn't know if she would see me again or my children. I had two children, a girl Lea, five, and boy Remy, three, which she loved so much.

This morning, May 4, 1999, I came to a letter dated 1958, a letter from my sister. In one part of the letter my sister is telling me how she was visiting a small town in Tunisia and she took my mother with her. While they were visiting, they would have to ride a ferry to cross the water and go to the other side of the beach. My mother loved it so much, she told my sister, "I wish this ferry will take me to Mathilda and her children." That made me feel sad, that she never saw them. The first time I went back to see my family it was after nine years, and I couldn't take my children with me because it was so expensive so I went alone. The second time I went back, I was going to take my last two children that she never knew. Two weeks before my departure, I received a telephone call telling me that my mother passed away.

 ## My Keepsake Quilt
Mary Lou Morgette

I have a double wedding ring quilt on one of my beds that is not used very much. It is special to me because I helped to piece it and also to quilt it. That was a common activity in our household as I was growing up.

The pieces of the quilt are made from scraps of material left from dresses we made. When my sisters and I were young, we looked at those pieces and identified each piece with the dress and person who wore it. I still like to try to remember whose dress that was. It has been more than fifty years since the quilt was made, so it's not so easy now.

Both of my grandmothers were quilt makers, and Mother had several aunts who liked to piece and put together quilts. Since Mother was a great believer that idle hands are the devil's workshop, we learned that fine art. We used a little piece of cardboard for the pattern and cut a lot of small pieces, which we stacked neatly until we had enough to make a square. Then we sewed them together, by hand. When we had enough squares, these were pieced together to make the whole quilt top. Now it was ready to be made into a real quilt. The back was stretched onto the quilting frames, which were suspended from the ceiling. Cotton batting was laid on this and then the top was added. This was all stretched very taut so that all layers would be smooth. This operation required a good-sized workspace, strong hands, and a lot of patience. Then one side was rolled so that there was a workable amount of quilt ready for the fine work of quilting. The needle was small and sharp and you had to take small stitches. The lines quilted usually followed the design made by all the pieces.

Quilts were usually put up in summer when there was not so much farm work to do. Mama's visits, as well as her sisters', took place during that period too. Mama lived in Fort Worth, Aunt Jessie and Aunt Ruth lived in the Panhandle, Aunt Annie lived in South Texas, and Aunt Allie lived in Munday. This was a reunion time for those ladies, and they had a lot to catch up on about what had happened since they had last seen each other. They gathered around the quilt, threaded their needles, and the visiting and stitching began. As my sisters and I joined in the quilting part we kept our mouths shut and our ears open. We learned a lot during those sessions as they talked about who had died, who had moved or married. They talked about who was expecting—never who was pregnant. That was a secret!

The quilting usually started around nine or ten in the morning and lasted until late afternoon, with a break for lunch and maybe a short rest. Some of those ladies dipped snuff, so that called for "spit cans." Every so often they would spit out that awful brown juice that built up in their mouths as they chewed on the snuff-laden "toothbrush." The toothbrush was a small twig taken from a peach or plum tree. It was chewed until the end was soft and shredded. When they got ready to take their first dip they chewed on that brush until it was moistened, then dipped it into the snuff glass until it was loaded. Then it went into their mouth. Yuk! And double yuk if it was your job to empty the spit cans. And double-double yuk if someone kicked over the can. The younger ones were assigned cleanup duty.

By the time the ladies had got their visits out and headed off to visit somewhere else, they had made two or three quilts. These were distributed and put away for the coming cold weather. My double wedding ring quilt was made during one of those sessions. It is a treasure for more than one reason, not the least of which is the knowledge that it was made by the loving hands of three generations.

The Legacy of the Two Lauras
Sue Kinney

The dilapidated old box still sits high up on my closet shelf (albeit a different closet), just as it did the day I first spied it. What is it about a five-year-old and the mystery of an unopened box, quite out of reach of little hands longing to explore its contents?

"Mommy," I shouted, "Come here quick!" Always obliging to her only daughter's whims, Mother appeared quickly at my door. "What is it?"

"That box," I squealed, "what's in that box on my top shelf?" It might have been Christmas for all the excitement it generated.

Mother reached for the box. I could hardly contain myself. Slowly, she lifted the lid, and we found inside the most beautiful patchwork quilt top I had ever seen. Bright colors danced in rainbow array radiating out into ever widening circles of lavender and blue and green and yellow. Almost immediately I spotted the red and white print. "That looks like my dress that I outgrew last year!"

And it was. Calico from aprons long worn out, bits and scraps of material left from whatever project my Granny, Laura, was working on, danced before my eyes. Santa could not have dreamed up a better surprise for me.

When I was through examining this new and unutterably beautiful treasure, Mother returned it to the box and placed it high on the closet shelf. It would lie there for months, sometimes years, before it was opened again, at those times when curiosity urged me to ask Mother to get the quilt down once more so I could see it. Perhaps it was so that I could make certain this link with the past was still intact.

Years went by and the quilt lay unfinished and temporarily forgotten. When my mother died, I found it among her possessions. "One day," I mused, "I am going to finish that quilt," but procrastination reigned, and the box took up residence on my closet shelf once again.

Then one day another Laura took charge, as she often does. "Mother, give me that quilt top, and I'll see about getting someone to finish it." She took it away and months passed with no mention of Granny's quilt. Christmas 1997 came, and a large, mysterious package appeared under the tree. Still like a child at Christmas, I couldn't wait for it to yield its surprise. I tore open the brightly wrapped box and slowly lifted the lid.

I was not disappointed. Granny's quilt lay before me, now bound and edged and carefully quilted, the subdued backing and border taking nothing away from the bright and dancing colors of the top.

And so it was that another Laura, born five months after her great-grandmother's death, had brought to fruition the task begun some sixty years earlier.

Mama's Writings
Irene Luedke

I treasure Mama's writings. They are a special link to my past. Mama and Papa, my maternal grandparents, reared my brother George and my sister Bettye (now Glass) and me, from my birth. Her writings began before I was born, with references beginning in 1929. She took the time to reflect on important events and to record them. As a child, I noticed Mama taking out her book to add an address of a dear one or to refer to a bit of information she had saved there.

Her writings were varied. They spoke of times of great joy, courage, and despair. Frequently, they were in the form of a prayer. She spoke about family trips in the Buick to Sutherland Springs, near San Antonio, to visit Aunt Kathleen's (Williams) family. She wrote about family holidays and parties. Christmas 1931, she reported, "My own dear husband gave his 'Ole Lady' a lovely radio."

Mama loved her grandchildren and recorded their happenings. "Today, August 21, 1940, a tiny bit of loveliness came to Maurine and Curly. God guide that precious life into paths of righteousness." That was Marilyn Sue, my cousin, their second born. Doris Jean, Carole Ann, and Rebecca Ruth are her sisters. We grandchildren played together most days. Those were times when children lived close by their parents. Two daughters lived in homes next to Mama, Aunt Maurine Menear and my mother. Two other daughters lived in town. They were Aunt Bennie Smith and Aunt Catherine (Blue Eyes) Howell. Aunt Sweetie (Cordellia Disch) lived in Dallas. Since there were eleven children in my grandparents' family, there were many references to happenings among them all, also. Papa's Geisendorff and Mama's Miller families were frequent entries. Even Great-grandmother Miller was present in the early writings.

Since most of the writings were done during the years my brother, sister, and I were living at home, many references are made to us. Mama recorded how much our school supplies cost; every pencil and tablet was itemized. She reported a trip Papa and I took to town to buy my violin case. She took note of our height and weight on birthdays. Our shot record was there. The course of each childhood disease was recorded in detail. "Betty Jean took the mumps Sunday, May 10, 1936. Just 21 days later, May 31, George took them. Neither was what you would call sick, though jaws of both were really swollen. George is comical looking. Wish I had a picture of him." "January 6, 1938, paid to Dr. Sutton $2.00 for Totsy [me], she was taking whooping cough."

A very big day for Mama: "July 20, 1936, I voted today for the primary July 25, as we plan to leave tomorrow for Sutherland Springs. Dad and I voted. This was my first time to vote." Another interesting entry dated 1932: "An autogiro was at our airport today, January 5." According to the dictionary, an autogiro, trademarked in 1923, is a rotary wing aircraft that employs a propeller for forward motion and a freely rotating rotor for lift.

Notations regarding Mama's quilt making: "Put star quilt together in June 1930." "Began the Roman Cross quilt in June, completed the block in July 1930." "Began my Dutch Girl quilt in November 1930." "Began my hexagon quilt December 2, 1930, finished December 5, 1931. Didn't sew a stitch on it from April 10 until November 4, 1931." "Began Japanese Fare quilt on March 12, 1932." "Quilted my wedding ring quilt for Minnie Florence, December 4 to 22, 1933."

Mama described the planting of the garden. She had petunias, hyacinths, roses, wild yellow jasmines, zinnias, snapdragons, marigolds, nasturtiums, dahlias, sweet peas, mums, African daisies, calendulas, periwinkles, night-blooming cape jasmines, statice (an herb), sunflowers, sweet violets, verbenas, and gladiolas. She described the daily plantings of the strawberry garden in October and November and the "very inclement weather." Their vegetable garden included onions, cauliflower, cabbage, tomatoes, cucumbers, sweet potatoes, corn and butter beans, Kentucky Wonder beans, pole and bush beans.

Mama described dry ice: "There is a plant in Mexico that ships dry ice to the United States. It is made from gas from oil wells. A piece weighing, say 20 lbs, in the hot sun for 24 hours, there will still be ice. . . ." She gave a remedy for alcoholism: "If a teaspoonful of compound tincture of cinchonine is taken before each meal, the desire of alcoholics will gradually disappear." Also, remedies for acne: "The face should be steamed night and morning and massaged with a Turkish towel. Castile soap should be used to cleanse the skin and sulfur salve should be applied each night."

Mama described several severe weather situations, such as long droughts and extreme wet spells. She wrote about a "terrible hurricane hitting Tampico, Mexico, September 25, 1935." Two days later, "No news, the anxiety is nerve-wracking. Our boy is there. Oh God, thy will be done." The next day, "Had a telegram from my boy, safe after a terrible hurricane. Don't worry, love." That was from Uncle Albert or Uncle Ernest. There were notations about the war and relatives serving in it. This quote from Uncle Otto Geisendorff: "So grieve not, mother o'mine, for that wandering son of thine. Let not worry gray your hair. The God above who is the essence of love is protecting me with His care."

In 1932, she told of the 1929 six-cylinder, four-door Buick sedan given to Mama by Uncle Boy (Henry). She wrote, "It is in excellent condition, the party who had owned it before us, took great pride in the appearance and care of his car, and I so hope we can do equally as well. We thought it was wonderful for our Boy to present us with a gift so nice as this car, and I do hope Dad will consent for me to learn to drive it. I want to so badly feel the thrill of driving it all by myself. . . ." I don't believe Mama ever got that wish to learn to drive. Several car wrecks were described in detail. The February 25, 1934, accident resulted in Mama's back injury. "The first thing I knew was Fred (Papa) and Benin tugging at me to know if I could get up. Oh, the horror of those few minutes before we got out and kindhearted men set the car up." On March 28, 1938, "License bought for Buick, $ 11.10." On April 1, 1941, "The old bus, 1934 eight-cylinder Buick will be in other hands. Fred has decided at last that he shouldn't drive and, too, it is so worn and isn't so safe anymore. But it has given us lots of pleasure, a good old car."

Mama entered family deaths, including that of my mother and father. "Wednesday, July 11, 1934. Our Heavenly Father saw fit to take our darling Girlie, Minnie Florence, and her precious baby [me] is mine, dad's and mine. God help us to do for

these dear little ones. Frank [my dad] came to us with his moth-
erless babies, the only home he has now." [He was orphaned as
a small child.] Of my father's death: "Frank (Arthur Chute) was
taken home in the morning of February 15, Wednesday. . . .
Took him to the hospital. There was little hope for him from
the beginning. Everything was done that could be done, but
the Grim Reaper won at 9:45 Sunday, February 19, 1939. We
miss him." He died of pneumonia.

Many references are made to Papa's illnesses and Mama's
struggle to comfort and protect him. Sunday, March 31, 1941,
Papa's blood pressure was 286 and Dr. Wilson ordered him to
bed for two weeks. Friday, April 18, 1941: "Fred had to go to
bed again, the 'spells' were numerous." September 25, 1941:
"Really think he had a stroke, for he is almost helpless. I have
to feed him again, as he can't use his hand."

Papa never fully recovered, but was able to go to the grocery, to town (Beaumont, Texas), and enjoy his grandchildren
and great-grandchildren. Frederick William Geisendorff, born
April 5, 1871, died November 19, 1952. My son Bryan Eugene
Syler was born the year of Papa's death on July 9, 1952. Mama
(Corinne Miller Geisendorff) was born October 16, 1873, and
died October 27, 1957, with diabetes. My son Kyle Lee Syler
was born June 11 of that year. Renee Syler Swank, my daughter, born September 7, 1968, came some years later. The hope
of this writing is that through me, my children will know my
Mama and Papa.

 The Other Side of Fifty
Betty Poe Howard

It's been a long time since I had my fiftieth birthday—twenty-
one years to be exact. I now have two offspring who are in their
fifties—a daughter who just had her fiftieth birthday, and a son
who is fifty-one. My almost fifteen-year-old granddaughter remarked yesterday that her mother didn't look fifty years old,

and questioned me to see if I agreed. She also wondered about her stepfather, who in her mind "only looked about forty-six years old" when he, too, is fifty. There was some concern in her voice that her parents were getting "old." If you don't look fifty, somehow you are escaping that fact of age. I agreed with her that both were not only young-looking, but were young, period. Explaining my view from the other side of fifty was new to me, when talking to a fifteen-year-old. I can remember thinking that fifty was really getting up there in age, and deep inside me I find that I still have that inner feeling. I have to tell myself that this is not a fact of life today. I know this is a time that can be the beginning of the best years of life.

I vividly remember a sermon given by a friend of ours on "Turning Fifty-five." His first thoughts about turning fifty-five were a bit negative. He saw himself going down that highway of life and all he could see was one of those big fifty-five-mile-per-hour highway signs at the top of the hill, and it was downhill from then on! The sermon became a very humorous self-examination. Thinking about what really was ahead for him and the challenges he faced, he became increasingly positive, and of course he ended the sermon on a note of excitement as to what lay ahead in his unknown future.

Milestones mark our journey down the highway of life, and I can look back now and have a great time visualizing these high points and some low points. Age fifty was a time in my life when I found myself with very few responsibilities or worries about kids or security in life. I had my own business, I had grandchildren, I still had a loving husband, and I had many friends and acquaintances. I had a beautiful home in a small community of Claremont, California, near enough to the mountains to visit them often and near enough to the ocean to experience the sun and sea. Life for me was beautiful.

I never have thought age fifty was a "turning point" in my life because as I grew older I appreciated all of my birthdays. How lucky I was to have another year on this earth. It's hard sometimes to see the day that has just passed as a horrible experience in life, as we all have those days. But I look at each morning as another chance to experience life to the fullest, and I try to live that day as the only day I have left. I've always tried to do what I can to make the world a better place. Your attitude toward life is what really counts. Every age is special, and in my memory, I can't think of one age that was better than all the rest!

If you are ever asked how old you are, just remember, there are really three ages: your chronological age, your physical age, and your mental age. Each can be very different from the others and in the big scheme of things, the chronological age can be the least important.

 A Letter to a Young Person
Marthanne Luzader

Dear Young Person,

Loss is inevitable. Somehow I got the idea early on that everything would stay the same. From the time I was ten months old until I was nine, I lived in the same house. It was the house my mother grew up in, as did her mother before her.

It was a great loss to me when we moved across town. I can see now that I gained new friends and did not really lose the old ones.

I remember moving to Cincinnati and feeling tragically far away from my family. My father came to visit, and I cried when he left. As I watched the car drive away, taking him back to Texas, I remember thinking, "I'm so glad I love someone enough to feel this way." I think now that had I understood and accepted that life changes constantly and that some changes mean loss, I might not have been so devastated every time I suffered the loss of neighborhood. Movement through life means new places, new people, new experiences every day. I always thought I could and should stop the movement and freeze some sort of perfection in time and place. Now I don't think it works that way. Life happens. You pay attention and ask God for instructions.

Happiness is possible. I used to think that happiness was the natural state of human beings, so when I was not happy, I figured something terrible was going on and I could and should fix it immediately. It's a difficult idea to shake. Maybe that was my Momma's idea. I remember her saying, "You either have to laugh or cry!" I think I got the idea that I was supposed to be happy and not angry or sad.

What I think now is that feelings are nature's way of telling us what's good for us. When something happens that you don't like, you quite naturally get sad or mad. Your feelings are about you, and you have to figure out what they mean sometimes before you know what's best to do. But it's always good to feel your feelings and express them. It's not good to get lost in them.

Feelings happen. You pay attention and ask God for instructions. Generally, that'll make you happy.

Happy Trails,
An Old Person

 "I Wish You Could Have
Known My Grandma"
Evelyn Simon

My dearest grandchildren,

If you don't know anything else about me, know one thing —you will always have my unconditional love. Although it's exciting to be able to see you excel in school, music, sports, whatever, my greatest reward would be to see each of you grow into moral, responsible, caring adults, with a love for God, neighbor, and country.

Here are a few insights I've amassed during my many years. Stand tall for what you believe in and be your own person. Always take responsibility for your actions, no matter how painful the outcome. Treat others as you would want to be treated, with kindness and respect. Always maintain a keen sense of humor and don't sweat the small stuff. (Now, where have I heard that before?) Be assertive, not aggressive. Let common sense prevail over pride. Always maintain a positive attitude and smile a lot, whether you feel like it or not. Remember what Abe Lincoln always said: "You're only as happy as you make up your mind to be." Set goals and be prepared to sacrifice to attain them. When problems do occur in your life (and trust me, they will), don't react hastily. Give the situation a lot of thought. Accept your current reality. Choose to create your vision and take action to make your vision a reality. In other words, don't stew over things you cannot change.

My heart would swell with pride if I could hear the next generation say: "I wish you could have known my grandma—she was an important part of my life and had a big influence on me."

Biographical Notes

Biographical notes were written by OWL Circle participants or their survivors and edited for publication here. Several women whose memoirs appear in the book did not respond to a request for biographical information.

Nadeane Walker Anderson lives in Austin with her cat Josephine and many fond memories. A native of East Texas, she wrote for *Stars and Stripes* during World War II in Paris, Berlin, and Vienna and is currently searching for a publisher for her late husband's wartime diaries. Addicted to crosswords, *Jeopardy*, and decorative crafts, she does Tai Chi, reads avidly, and keeps in touch with a few remaining friends and kin internationally through e-mail.

Minnie Ree Baccus, now deceased, was born in Texas in the year 1910. Her parents moved her to Oklahoma as an infant in a covered wagon. She became one of the first female postmasters in Oklahoma after the Burns Flat appointment became available due to World War II, and she held that position for thirty-four years. She is survived by two children, six grandchildren, and five great-grandchildren.

Agatha Barbay, born and raised in Baton Rouge, Louisiana, is a wife and mother of four. Her husband Lawrence, a retired U.S. Air Force officer, served his country for twenty-three years.

They have retired in Austin, Texas. She writes, "We give thanks to God each and every day for His bountiful blessings."

Bobbye Jo Barker retired after spending twenty years in health-care administration. Now that she is so busy with gardening and grandkids, Bobbye wonders how she found time to go to work. She fills the remaining hours with reading, writing, music, and as little housework as possible.

Ruby Varnon Bishop lives in Georgetown, Texas, with her husband Don. She has come to writing late in life, after raising four children, and enjoys drawing on her rich background of life in six foreign countries. She spends much time in volunteer work and is a dedicated Rotarian. She is a sometime gardener and avid reader. She shares her quiet time with her cats Tuffy and Smoky.

Lucy A. Boyea is the founder and director of St. Matthew's Senior Activity Center in Austin, Texas. She is the mother of three children and grandmother of five. A registered nurse by profession, with advanced degrees in Health Education and Health Administration, Lucy feels truly blessed by her ministry, now in its eighth year.

Martha (Marty) Brian grew up on the prairie of western Kansas, attended Kansas State University, and worked in the oil industry. She married early and had four children. She was employed in Washington, D.C., and moved back to Texas to help her husband through seminary, by working at KTBC television and radio. She experienced life as the wife of an Episcopal priest who served in three different churches. She spent the next few years alone; then she remarried and moved to Florida, where she studied art and learned sailboat racing and cruising. She and her husband Pat retired to Sun City, near Georgetown, Texas, where she attends classes, enjoys dancing and tap dancing, and has organized a spiritual growth group.

Carole Burke is an attorney with a master's degree in social work from UT Austin, adding the counseling dimension to her work. She lives in the country near Georgetown, Texas, with her husband Rod, two Irish setters, and a cat. Her son Adam attends college in Austin.

Helen Burnette works at the University of Texas and doesn't plan to retire for several more years. She lives with her daughter; her other children and grandchildren live nearby. Her work, family, church activities, and meditation fill her days to the brim.

Helen Greer Burton worked as a travel agent after her three children were grown. She was blessed with the opportunity to travel to remote places in the world and take some of her best friends with her. Her most memorable trip was visiting Xian in China and walking alongside the thousands of terra-cotta soldiers, life-sized warriors uncovered from their burial stations. She is now retired and lives at the Heritage at Gaines Ranch in Austin, Texas.

Joann Bynum and her second husband lived in Chapala, Mexico, for two years. Following that, they moved to San Antonio so the children could finish school. Having enjoyed the Hill Country, they bought a house in Wimberley, Texas. Joann raised Yorkshire terriers for twenty years and now has four Pomeranians to keep her busy. Her two daughters, eleven grandchildren, and ten great-grandchildren live in Indiana, while another daughter and three children live near Wimberley.

Pauline Carey was born in Missouri on August 5, 1921. She has one daughter, two granddaughters, and five great-grandchildren. She and her husband moved to Austin in 1982 to be near the family. She volunteers now for RSVP.

Oleta Cates was born December 11, 1920, in the town of Corn Hill, Texas, which no longer exists. She was married and lived in Dallas until 1969, and now resides in Austin, where she does oil painting and grows roses as a hobby.

Patricia J. Click is a retired English and Drama instructor who grew up in the Texas Panhandle and began her teaching career in a one-room schoolhouse. She lived for many years in eastern New Mexico, where she and her husband raised their two daughters. Patricia taught English in the public schools and was part of the English and Drama departments at Eastern New Mexico University. She completed her teaching career on the Navajo Reservation in Arizona and is now enjoying her retirement in Austin.

Lavern Crawford wishes to thank OWL Circle facilitator Carolyn Blankenship, who led her Story Circle class in the writing of her memoirs. At the age of seventy-eight, Lavern realized that some of her experiences in life could be of interest to others. Lavern lives in Austin with her husband Melvin. They have two daughters and three grandchildren.

Joan H. Crews was a homemaker for forty-seven years, twenty-eight of which were spent moving with her military husband and three children. She loves to paint and sew, and since becoming a widow eight years ago, she has traveled abroad extensively.

Joyce A. Dehlin has lived most of her life on the high plains of North Dakota. She and her husband Glenn raised two daughters, a son, and several dogs. For sixteen years she served as program director, teacher, and counselor at a home for pregnant teens. She earned a master's degree just prior to her fiftieth birthday.

Kathryn Doggett is a retired real estate broker who lives with her husband Bill in Sun City. They have three children and six grandchildren. Kathryn enjoys walking, strength training, tap dancing, and being a part of the Sun City drill team. She is also very involved in the computer club and was instrumental in setting up a dozen investment clubs in Sun City.

Jeanie Forsyth is a book junkie who lives in Austin, Texas, with her husband of twenty-five years, Phil, in a house whose ample bookshelves long ago failed to accommodate her ever-increasing collection. A mother of four, she is a student of life and finds learning experiences still abundant in her seventy-fifth year. She loves laughter, music, friends, flowers, birds, new adventures, writing, comparing notes on aging with contemporaries (especially her sister Alice), listening to people's stories, and life itself, in all its joy and sadness.

Oma Gillis passed away at age ninety-two on November 4, 1999, in Austin, Texas. She was born in Union, Oregon, on March 7, 1907. She is survived by a sister, Mary Falconer, of Walla Walla, Washington, and a stepson and his wife, Robert and Annabelle Gillis of Austin.

When *Amparo González* learned to use a computer, this self-professed late bloomer discovered a new love, writing. Their travels during her husband's military career, rearing four children, and an avid love for nature have given her much to write about. Since settling in the Hill Country, this grandmother of two writes a daily log, stays busy with church activities, gardens, and writes long letters and e-mail to family and friends.

Patricia Gunderlach is a retired high school teacher who, along with her husband Bud, joined other Houston refugees in Wimberley, escaping the freeways and the crowds. Now she has the time to do volunteer work, read a compelling novel deep into the night, and socialize with friends.

Wanda Heath has been a Pennsylvanian, a Floridian, and now resides in Sun City, where she and her husband moved to be closer to their two sons and grandchildren. She is a retired high school teacher and medical office manager. She enjoys travel, camping, Bible study, amateur theater, tap dancing, sewing, cross-stitching, and gardening. She wonders how she ever found time to work!

Billie Grace Herring, Professor Emerita of Library and Information Science at the University of Texas, lives in Austin with her husband Jim and their two cats. She enjoys their four grandchildren, entertaining, travel, sleeping late, and listening to classical music. A collector of paperweights and baskets, she especially appreciates Native American and other folk art.

Erma Hiltpold is ninety-four years old. One of fourteen children, she grew up on the family farm in Caldwell County, Texas. She attended a two-room schoolhouse, studied journalism and English at Oklahoma University, and pursued creative writing at Pan Am University. She paints, has traveled throughout the United States and Mexico, and has played golf for many years. She lives in Austin.

Mary Holder is a widow who lives in Austin to be near her daughter and her family. She grew up in a small town during the Depression. She graduated from Texas Women's University, taught home economics and kindergarten, and worked as a junior chemist during the war. She enjoys reading, gardening, music, and family get-togethers.

Betty Poe Howard lives in Austin, continuing to learn in a Third Age program called LAMP (Learning Activities for Mature People) at the University of Texas. An avid traveler, dancer, writer, and social activist, she also enjoys her family of four adult children, nine grandchildren, and one great-grandchild.

Gayle Hunt has worked picking cotton on the farm as a child, raised two children, graduated from college at thirty-nine, and retired as director of a clinical microbiology laboratory. In retirement, she enjoys reading, mastering the computer, and traveling. She lives in Georgetown with her husband of fifty years.

Sherlie Hurwitz was born in Clovis, New Mexico, on April 30, 1923. She married her husband Alvin when he was serving as a private in the U.S. Army Air Force at Hondo, Texas, during World War II. They have two sons, a daughter, eight grandchildren, and one great-grandchild. Through the motivation and persistence of their children, all the immediate family has migrated over the years to Austin. Now seventy-seven, Sherlie is a member of a tap-dance group. When not dancing (almost never, these days) she pursues her lifelong goal of self-publishing her poems and other original writing, dating back to her childhood days, to leave as a legacy for her heirs. She writes: "Life is good, life is busy, and I feel very blessed to look into the mirror each morning and say, 'Yep! I'm still here!'"

Faye L. Kelly is a fourth-generation native Floridian now living in Austin, to be near her daughter. She is Professor Emerita of American University in Washington, D.C. In her salad days, she flew her own airplanes. Her other interests include jewelry making, sewing, and fishing.

Louise Kent is a mother of four daughters, grandmother of nine, and great-grandmother of six who takes great joy in her very supportive family. Louise moved to Austin in 1988, after retiring from a twenty-two-year career with the federal government in Washington, D.C.

Sue Kinney is a recently retired academic administrator and mother of three adult children. She has filled her time since retirement with travel, church work, refugee resettlement, and a myriad of other activities. Her future plans include writing about her experiences as a frontier wife living in a remote Alaskan Indian village, as well as collaborating on a history of her parish church.

Janie Kirkpatrick married in Cheyenne, Wyoming, had four children, graduated from the University of Texas at Austin, and taught school for twenty years. Janie is retired and recently moved to the hills west of Wimberley. She keeps busy with her husband, two dogs, walking, bird-watching, reading, and people-related activities.

Martha Knies, a native Texan born in Marlin, lives with her husband Ted in the scenic Hill Country village of Wimberley. In addition to her volunteer work with Keep Wimberley Beautiful, she is now a council person for the recently incorporated town. Her previous career included teaching English and serving as the librarian for fourteen years at Willis, Texas.

Bonnie Knipp was born in Hattiesburg, Mississippi, and has been married for forty years. Before her marriage, she worked at various jobs, and when her five children were young, volunteered in their schools and in PTA and church programs. Now, she serves as the facilitator for her church's Senior Friendship Group and volunteers in other church activities. She enjoys reading, making rosaries, cooking, and working crossword puzzles. She has six grandchildren.

Janine M. Koch grew up in Hannibal, Missouri. She married her childhood sweetheart forty-four years ago, and now has seven children and thirteen grandchildren. She does volunteer work with St. Vincent de Paul Society and spends quiet time at a river getaway in Kerrville with her family.

Katherine Koonce retired from teaching and working as an elementary school reading specialist in 1996. She and her husband moved to Sun City in 1997. Katherine is enjoying many activities in Sun City, including china painting, choral singing, a book club, and working out at the fitness center. She also volunteers at the Georgetown schools in the Partners in Education program and serves as an elder in the Community of Christ church. She enjoys travel, reading, playing Scrabble, and being with her family, which includes three children and four grandchildren.

Lorene B. Laird grew up and attended school in rural northwest Oklahoma, where she was valedictorian of her high school class. She graduated from Northwestern State University with a B.S. in Home Economics and Elementary Education. In 1942, she married Second Lieutenant Charles E. Laird and followed him during his twenty-year U.S. Air Force career. Lorene taught school for two years in Rome, New York, and for eighteen years in Austin. The Lairds have four sons, eight grandchildren, and three great-grandchildren. They are both retired and lead a busy life at the Heritage, a Senior Living Center in Austin.

Jean Leonard, a former school librarian and college librarian, retired with her mathematics professor husband from the State University of New York at Oneonta to Austin in 1982. After employment in retailing for several years, she retired again to do volunteer work and travel with her husband to visit their three sons and families living across the United States and in Europe. An invitation to submit a "memory story" to *The Outlook* (the monthly publication of the Jewish Community Center of Austin) led to a new adventure as a writer. Jean also enjoys aerobics, walking, music, reading, and her involvement in OWL Circle workshops.

Sarah Lichtman was born in 1920 in Poland, in Piotrkow Trybunalski. She finished her studies at a public school, which was attended only by Jewish children, then enrolled in a business school for three years. She was married after the war and lived in Germany for four years. In 1949 she came to the United States and lived in Milwaukee, Wisconsin, for over fifty years. For the past several years Sarah lived in Austin, near her daughter. She died on November 10, 2002.

Margaret C. Long is a retired social worker who moved to Austin to be near her daughter and granddaughters. Always a reader and writer, she is concentrating now on writing the story of her life and the lives of her ancestors for her own descendants.

Irene Luedke, a retired speech pathologist, lives in Georgetown. She enjoys her church, her neighborhood, her small group experiences, the gym, swimming, biking, and gardening. Irene's special interests are the healing ministry and mentoring teenage girls.

Marthanne Luzader moved from ingénue to crone with one foot in Austin and another on a farm in Williamson County, Texas. Born in 1933, she claims to carry the "Depression mentality" to new heights.

Pat Lyón is a wife of forty-three-plus years, mother of two sons, and grandmother of a boy and girl. After living in Venezuela for thirty years, she is enjoying country life in Wimberley. Pat is a gourmet cook and loves to read, embroider, and putter in her herb garden. She and her husband José are active in St. Mary's Parish in Wimberley and love to travel.

Betty Martin, a native of Houston, is the mother of four grown sons and eight grandchildren. She and her husband Jack have resided in Wimberley for the past twenty-two years. After serving in public education for twenty-three years, she retired to spend more time with her husband and grandchildren. Betty loves writing for her family and making family-legacy scrapbooks for each son as lasting reminders of their heritage.

Eula Rae McCown is a native Texan who has lived all over the world. She is a widow and has three sons and six grandchildren. Her hobbies are cooking, gardening, and handwork. She was recently married to her first boyfriend of fifty-six years ago. At the time of her participation in the OWL Circle Project, she served as Coordinator of Seniors at St. Louis Catholic Church in Austin.

Sarah McKinney was born in Stephens, Arizona, on October 15, 1932. She grew up in South Texas (in Alice and Corpus Christi) and has lived in Austin since 1967. A retired state employee, she is a widow with one son. She maintains her home for the convenience and comfort of her two Airedales.

Mathilda Mimun, born in Tunisia, immigrated to the United States and came to San Antonio in 1957. Now living in Austin, she is a semi-retired seamstress. She has four children and ten grandchildren.

Erin Colleen Moore grew up on the ranch with her three sisters. She attended the University of Texas at Austin and the University of Wisconsin in Madison. Her career was at M. D. Anderson Cancer Center, Houston, with research on cell growth and its controls. She has a retirement center apartment and enjoys her cat, her sister, and numerous nieces and nephews.

Mary Lou Morgette lives in Austin. She has two daughters and five grandchildren. Her enjoyment of writing was awakened late in her life. Sewing and travel to England with C. B., her husband, are just two of the activities that keep her busy during retirement. She is also involved in Bible studies at her church.

Dolores R. Muhich is a semi-retired businesswoman and former educator who lives in Austin with her cat Speckles. She has four adult children, twelve grandchildren, and three great-grandchildren. She taught at the high school, junior college, and university levels and was owner/manager of a small dormitory in Illinois before moving to Austin. She has published in several professional journals and is listed in *Who's Who*. In addition to managing her investments, she dances in competition, attends Scrabble tournaments, sings in the church choir, and keeps fit with yoga and workouts in the gym.

Jane R. Peppard was born Jane Frances Riddell, in Brooklyn, New York, in 1933. She received degrees in nursing from Boston University and in health care administration from Long Island University. After her husband died, she moved to Georgetown to be near her daughter Marita Therese and her two grandchildren. She takes classes at Senior University in Georgetown, watches the Red Sox on television, and attends the baseball games of the Round Rock Express.

Selah Rose is a retired nurse who is enjoying her life at Sun City. Mother of five and grandmother of twelve, she has been a caretaker all of her life. She is finally investing in her own well-being and creative talents, and loving her independence.

Val Jean Peters Schmidt is a mother of two sons, a grandmother of four, and a retired elementary school teacher. Born in the Lower Rio Grande Valley near Harlingen, this native Texan now resides in Austin. Precious things in her life today include family, home, friends, church, volunteer work, and gardening.

Grace B. Schmitt lived in New York until her marriage in 1949. After having children and making several moves, she settled in Austin in 1958. Grace, a librarian, developed a puppetry program for children at the Austin Public Library. Since retirement, she has volunteered her time for a number of charitable programs.

Jo Scudder spent eleven happy years as a rural mail carrier after moving to Wimberley twenty-five years ago. Now she enjoys swimming and watching football and baseball. Five grandchildren live next door. Divorced, she spends time at the bridge table and makes an occasional trip to the Texas coast.

Alice M. Short, a retired administrator, is a wife, a mother of five, and a grandmother of eleven who lives in Austin. She enjoys travel, "especially tooling around the country by automobile to visit longtime friends," bridge, and the friendship of many

Pat Simmons is a mother and a retired school counselor She grew up in Johnstown, Pennsylvania. After college, she moved to Texas, where she raised her four children and continued her career as a teacher and counselor. In retirement, she spends her time in travel, reading, Bible study, and needlework. She now resides in Georgetown with her husband Bob.

Marji Smith lives in a small town on the north shore of Lake Travis with her husband and two cats. After a successful electronics design career, she is now the director of the community's library. She has a keen interest in history and enjoys reading, nature, and lively conversation. A part-time writer, she is currently working on her first book.

Paula Stephens-Bishop is a dedicated writer who relocated to central Texas from the Panhandle in 1999. After hectic years in the Texas oil patch, she spent an adventurous year as a new bride on a Lampasas ranch. Paula resides in Georgetown with her husband Robert. Between family and writing, she says that her dreams are fulfilled.

Williene Smith Story, a native of East Texas and daughter of a real cowboy, spent early married years in Tyler and Nacogdoches, where she became a charter member of the Stone Fort Chapter of the Daughters of the Republic of Texas. She is a member of the Daughters of the American Revolution and is active in the Christian Church. Once considered a fair baker, she says, she is now more diligent in aquatic exercise than in housekeeping.

Ruby A. Taylor enjoys living with her cat Blondie, feeding wild birds, and driving for caregivers. Her hobbies include oil painting with the Municipal Art Guild and bird-watching. She has been a widow since 1987, after twenty-seven years as an Air Force wife. Her only son also lives in Austin.

Eileen C. Titus was born and raised in England. In 1945, she married an American serviceman and joined him the following year in Massachusetts. Enjoying New England and the people she met, she put down roots and became a U.S. citizen. Retirement brought another move, this time to Austin, where she and her husband Sidney enjoy the warm climate. Now a great-grandmother, Eileen takes pleasure in her garden, bird-watching, water color painting, and being with her family.

Rose Vrba is a mother, grandmother, and great-grandmother who came from Nebraska twenty years ago to be near her family. She was a country schoolteacher, a mother and home-maker, owner and operator of a women's dress shop, and a newspaper correspondent. She is ninety years old and spends her time teaching Bible, volunteering, crocheting, and reading. Her greatest treasure is her family of six children, seven grandchildren, and seven great-grandchildren.

Mary G. Warren lives in Austin with her precious golden retriever Alexander. Mary, an Austin resident for thirty-five years, is active in volunteer work, has a part-time job, swims daily at Barton Springs Pool, and plays bridge "as often as possible," she says. Her two grown sons and one grandson live close enough to visit regularly. Football season is family time at Mary's.

Janice Wilkins is a retired teacher who lives with her husband Gene in Sun City. She now has the time to enjoy the things she loves to do: reading, nurturing friendships, participating in

Bible study, playing with grandchildren, traveling, swimming, and allowing some hidden talents to surface.

Pat McKenzie Williamson is from West Texas, where her father was in oil-field construction. After spending many years in Corpus Christi and Dallas, she now lives in Wimberley, close to her children, grandchildren, and her great-grandchild. She and her husband Jack married three years ago, and Pat has been fulfilling a lifelong dream by traveling all of the United States and the world. At home, she is active with family and friends, reading, and enjoying life.

Jean Wyllys was born in England and came to the United States as a young woman. Now retired, she lives in Austin, as do her four children and five grandchildren. She enjoys traveling in Italy with her sister.

Marilyn Zimmerman was born in 1931 in Pittsburgh, Pennsylvania, and moved to Springfield, Massachusetts, when she was four. After finishing public school in Massachusetts, she went to college in Pittsburgh, where she met her husband. They moved to Sheboygan, Wisconsin, where her husband entered the family's fourth-generation printing business. They have three children, and their son now owns the printing company. They moved to Texas in 1998.

About the Story
Circle Network

Women will starve in silence until new stories are created
which confer on them the power of naming themselves.
Sandra Gilbert and Susan Gubar

The Story Circle Network (SCN) was founded in 1997 to encourage and support women memoirists. A nonprofit organization funded by membership dues, programs, and gifts, SCN has
members around the United States and in several foreign countries. The Network is guided by a board of directors that plans
and oversees its programs and activities. These include chapters,
writing and reading circles, an award-winning web site, a major
women's on-line book review site, a quarterly printed journal,
monthly e-mail newsletters, on-line writing classes, and many
special projects, such as the ongoing OWL Circle Project and
books like *With Courage and Common Sense*. In the Austin,
Texas, area, SCN offers classes, workshops, retreats, and con-
ferences, together with special outreach programs. The organization's first national conference was held in 2002; the second
is planned for 2004. The OWL Circle Project continues to offer workshops in the Austin area; the Project's Workbook and
Facilitators' Manual are now available to the public through the
Story Circle office or the OWL Circle web site.

Information about membership and programs may be obtained from the Network's office or at its web sites.

The Story Circle Network
P.O. Box 500127
Austin, TX 78750-0127
phone: 512-454-9833
e-mail: storycircle@storycircle.org
www.storycircle.org
www.owlcircle.com